UNDIAGNOSED

A JOURNEY OF HOPE

Randy Beal

Disclaimer

I have tried to recreate events, locales, and conversations from my memories of them. In order to maintain their anonymity in some instances I have changed the names of individuals and places. I may have changed some identifying characteristics and details such as physical properties, occupations and places of residence.

Trademarks

All of the following words, phrases, and facilities mentioned in this book are registered trademarks®:

NY Jets, ALCO, Kentucky Fried Chicken, Mountain Dew, Cheetos, Atkins diet, Bears, Oprah, CAT scan, Hooters, Thera-Band, IHOP, Denny's, White Sox, MarianJoy, Mayo Clinic

This book is dedicated to
Dad, Matt, Tom, & Lawrence

CONTENTS

Acknowledgments

I want to give acknowledgment to all the doctors, nurses, therapists, drivers, transporters, and office staff who have helped to care for me through the years. To my family and friends, thanks for helping me during each stage of the illness. Michael, thanks for all your help on this project and for rocking the cover design. Aunt Sandy, thanks for believing in me and my dream. The biggest acknowledgment is to Bob: without you this book never could have been written.

UNDIAGNOSED

PART ONE: UNDIAGNOSED

MY DREAM

I had a dream on September 2, 2006, in which I saw the Sears Tower on TV. A huge white blanket draped one side of this Chicago landmark and helicopters flittered on and off the screen. Something BIG was happening, and I felt compelled to be there.

The next instant, I was there, in a wheelchair, being pushed up the last few internal steps of the Tower onto the roof. Now I realized what the hub-bub was all about. Chicago Mayor, Richard Daley, was perched on the ledge of the building, about to throw himself over.

I knew I had to do something so I began talking to him. He told me that he had just been diagnosed with cancer and wanted to end his life. What better way for Chicago's mayor to make a grand exit than off the side of the iconic Sears Tower? I don't remember exactly what I said to Mayor Daley to talk him out of it. Perhaps I told him things I imagine you would tell a person about to leap off a building. Things like: "You don't have to jump. You have so much to live for. You can beat this;

many people do."

Whatever it was, it worked. He left the ledge, crisis averted, and I was elated. I had saved the life of the mayor of Chicago! I turned to see droves of people lined up to jump next and for multitudes of reasons. One at a time, I talked each one off the ledge and continued to do so until I woke abruptly, wide-eyed and marveling at how vivid the dream had been.

I'm not normally a vivid dreamer, and I'll certainly never forget this one. In many ways, the dream captures my purpose in writing this book. I want to be able to help people, no matter their social standing or background, who have reached a similar point of despair, no matter the reason. I want to be able to share my story in hopes that something I have to say will spark renewed hope and the will to go on. I've talked myself off the ledge many times. Now I want to help you do the same.

A Stupid Teenager

I'm not quite sure where to start. I struggled with this for months when I first contemplated writing a book and it got me absolutely nowhere. So I'm going to start with now: a blog entry from early 2007.

> What a feeling! It's been awhile, but today we went walking. I've done a lot of standing and other exercises to help with control and strength, but today I just knew it was time to go for it. To date the most I've walked without braces was 6 steps. Today I walked 14 steps, took a break, and did the exact same 2 more times, and finished with 9 steps, a grand total of 51. At one point while walking, I got a huge smile on my face and my mom thought I was going to take off running. The steps I took today felt so good. They really helped my psyche.

As you can tell, I was thrilled that I was able to take 51 steps, without braces. Even better, check out the following week's entry:

> If you can do it in your mind, you can do it in body. I set a goal of 30 continuous steps and today I did 31. That was on the way to a grand

3

total of 202. Just 11 days ago I could only do 51 with good amounts of rest between each round of steps. The most I could do continuously was 14. Whew what a difference. Talk about being on a high. And I feel like I could do more too.

Two hundred and two steps in a single day! That was monumental. It made me want to set the bar even higher. So I set the next single-day step goal to 300 and was excited about the day when I would walk again, unassisted.

Funny that the task of telling my story was so daunting to me when I thought of everything I've been through from the beginning. But starting like I did with where I am right now gave me just the jump start I needed. I think the first step out of any seemingly hopeless situation has got to be taking an assessment of where you currently are. It's an assessment that you have to repeat over and over at each stage of recovery. Knowing where you stand (or sit in my case) is critical to knowing where you will go next.

You've probably gathered by now that I'm confined to a wheelchair and am only now starting to take steps again. How I came to be in this state is a long and strange story.

Prior to 2000, I was your typical stupid teen-aged male: healthy, active, and enjoying life. I was a football lineman for our high school team and was pretty ingrained into football culture and the parties and popularity that go along with it. During off-season, the football team would do a lot of power lifting to stay in shape and I got into it enough to officially join the power-lifting team my junior and senior years. Our team took 2nd place at a local power-lifting meet and 1st place the next year. I never thought twice about how great it felt to run across the football field or to stretch my legs out after an aggressive lift. I took these things for granted, as most teenagers do.

Like most teenagers, I also started to think about ways to get out of Dodge. I think about travel a lot now, but back then it was relatively new to me. I had heard of exotic places beyond the five states that bordered my home state, but had never ventured outside that circle of safety. So in 1998, I jumped at the chance to go on a summer mission trip with my church youth group to Mexico for 10 days.

Our group of twenty teen-agers, plus two chaperones, flew first to St. Louis to catch a connecting flight to Mexico City. This was my first-ever flight, and I pretty·much kept the air sickness bag glued to my face. Turbulence was not a part of my vocabulary back then. But I, at least, felt a sense of accomplishment just getting through that first leg of the flight.

In St. Louis, I was singled out from the group as the only one without proper documentation. (I had a copy of my birth certificate and not the real deal.) This meant I had to stay an extra night alone in St. Louis, get my parents to overnight the birth certificate, and fly alone to Mexico City the next day. Not the greatest first travel experience, but again I enjoyed the sense of accomplishment at being on my own, if only for a day.

I rejoined the group without further incident. In Mexico City, we split up and lodged with various hosts from a local church. I and two other compadres were matched with a young single guy who lived in a multi-level home. He gave us a tour of Mexico City by night and helped us order tacos from street vendors. They actually cooked the taco meat in a hollowed out tree trunk. I felt very suave and sophisticated.

To give you an idea of my physical state at the time, we actually did some pretty strenuous work on that trip. Part of our mission was to help build a rehab center. I remember busting my back digging a ditch in some steamy weather and fuming inside because I felt like I was doing the lion's share of the physical labor. I threatened to knock some heads with a shovel, but our gracious chaperone talked me out of it.

It wasn't all hard labor, though. We got to visit

some of the pyramid ruins outside Mexico City. We had made a pact beforehand that the entire group would climb the pyramid once we got there. I'm not a fan of heights; in fact, I'm a sworn enemy of all lofty places. (I once scored sweet front row seats to an Olympic event because my friends cited my "vertigo" issues to the ushers.) As you can imagine, I tried to worm my way out of climbing that pyramid, but the peer pressure was intense. The group egged me on and I wanted to prove to them and to myself that I could do it.

And I did. I was quite excited--still scared, but wanting to yell, "In your face!" to everyone who had pushed me to do it. We spent a bit of time at the top, and I took the opportunity to open up my pocket Bible, roulette fashion, and see what it had to say. It was a liberally paraphrased version, and the passage said something to the effect of, "Stop being such a wuss!" I must admit this took a bit of the wind out of my sails.

I look back fondly on times like this when I was healthy enough to dig ditches and climb mountains. Some memories are more difficult than others, but in general, instead of pining for the good ol' days, I look forward to even greater adventures in the future. I'm trying to take that "wuss" verse to heart.

The Mexico trip whetted my appetite for more

travel.   When another mission trip opportunity came up in November of 2000, I was SO there. This time it was to Africa and things were about to change.

Africa Mission

If you had asked me if I could ever picture myself traveling to Africa, I would have given you a strange look. But when one of my pastors asked me to join an Africa mission trip, I said yes without hesitation. Since I was somewhat of a last minute addition to the trip, there wasn't much time to prepare. I had to get my first passport and the multiple vaccinations the trip required. I got the vaccinations at an infectious disease center. I was more worried about the pain from the shot itself than the possibility of catching a debilitating virus (you can add needles to my "not-a-fan-of" list). Little did I suspect at the time of the vaccination that I would one day be back at the center for a far different reason.

A few weeks before the trip, I was at work at my family business when my left eye started tearing up. I also noticed that I was having some difficulty talking. I could move my mouth some, but half of it wasn't cooperating. Shortly after that, the entire left side of my face went numb—to the point that I was actually drooling on myself.

I saw my family doctor the next day when the

symptoms continued. He diagnosed the condition as Bell's palsy. Bell's palsy is a type of facial paralysis that is temporary in nature and is the result of either trauma or damage to one or two of a person's facial nerves. My doctor prescribed steroids, of which I only took a few doses. Thankfully by the time we took off for Uganda, all symptoms were gone.

The first flight was to London. I was a bit unnerved by those TV monitors that charted our flight path and kept hovering over the ocean for hours at a time, but otherwise, my first overseas flight proved uneventful. I felt a little odd when we landed, like a cold was coming on, but was soon distracted by all the sights and sounds London has to offer. We had one full day of rampant tourism before the Uganda branch of the trip, and we took full advantage of it by visiting the standard hot spots: Big Ben, Buckingham Palace, the London Eye. I gave fish and chips a try—disgusting!

While we were hanging about Buckingham, one of the guys in our group, George, was particularly intrigued by the Queen's Guard and their vow of silence. George thought he would succeed where so many others had failed and embarked on a campaign of taunts and jeers to draw one of the guards out. His campaign was so obnoxious and persistent that it actually paid off. The guard motioned him into an alley and, setting aside that famed British stiff upper lip, delivered a severe tongue-lashing that George and everyone else on the trip wouldn't soon forget.

Our final flight to Kampala offered incredible views from the plane, first of the Alps and then of the Sahara desert. The majesty of those scenes contrasted sharply with the smallness of the airport. I was amazed that the steps had to be rolled out to the plane and that the entire airport was not much bigger than a motel. Machine-gun-toting guards constantly patrolled the area, adding to my discomfort, but we made it out of the airport and to our hotel without any incident.

The next day, we caravanned into a more rural area in several SUVs. The trip was long and treacherous; I can only describe it as white water rafting on a dirt road. I marvel that we didn't flip over. We arrived safely and settled in with the work of our mission, which included teaching Sunday School to groups of village children. One of my primary tasks was to provide audio-visual support to a large group of pastors. I lugged the projector to a conference, only to discover that a power cord hadn't been packed. I felt that sickening, sinking feeling as I realized this and explained it to the group. We managed to rig something up in time for the first meeting, but I still felt terrible about the whole thing.

Within a day or so of that, I felt a more literal sickening. It started with an intense headache— borderline migraine—and progressed to puking, diarrhea, and absolute loss of energy. What was worse is that I became dehydrated. I knew better than to drink from the tap, though I was tempted.

The loss of energy resulted in a profound and seemingly insatiable need to sleep. I missed several day's worth of activities with the group because I slept through them. A few times I dragged myself out to a church service. You haven't experienced a worship service until you've experienced one in Africa. They're intense, to say the least, and can often include non-traditional expressions of joy, such as lifting up folding chairs over your head and twirling them around. Despite the loud singing, rigorous shouts of praise, fervent dancing, running, jumping, and chair twirling, I'd sleep through most of these services, just dropping my head where I sat. I usually had to be woken up at dismissal.

During one of our trips back to the hotel, I struck up a conversation with our driver about how I was feeling.

He said, "It sounds like African sleeping sickness."

"What's that?" I asked.

"It's when you go to sleep and never wake up" he answered.

"That's called death," I returned. For some reason this amused him and he laughed and laughed over it.

My stay in Africa was nearing a close and I still was no better. Three of us, George, Steve, and I, had to leave for the States early, so we headed once again to the airport in two vehicles. One vehicle carried the passengers and most of our bags, while the other carried overflow luggage. My backpack containing my passport happened to be on the overflow vehicle. Our plan was for both SUVs to meet first at the hotel and then at the airport. Along the way, the SUVs got separated and ours arrived at the hotel first. We waited patiently for the other SUV until we could wait no more.

Once again I found myself in a situation where I was the only one who didn't have the proper rites of passage. I suggested to our host pastor that he could pull some strings with the airport authorities to get me on that plane. He couldn't offer me that but he did share his faith in God with me.

"Go to the airport by faith. God will make a way."

Sure enough, the other vehicle was waiting there, just in time for my flight and with exactly what I needed.

Sometimes on our life journey we simply misplace our passports. We find ourselves lacking what we need to break away from a place of suffering to a place of peace.

This is a stressful and frightening place to be. The certainty and weight of obstacles in the path looms ominously and larger than life here. I have learned that it pays to lunge forward toward your goal, as if you already have what you need. More often than not, your passport awaits you on the other side.

We were all motivated to get back home quickly. On the London to Chicago flight, the pilot announced that flight would take about nine hours. George woke me to repeat the captain's assessment.

I said, "I asked God to get us there quicker," and fell back asleep. The next thing I remember was George waking me again.

"Randy!" he shouted, shaking me, "the pilot just announced that we caught a strong tailwind on the way back and made it in record time!" He and Steve were shocked. I just smiled. Perhaps the faith of that pastor had rubbed off a little on me.

For several weeks after my return, I remained

extremely sleepy and experienced several headaches. I was able to function somewhat normally but felt more run-down than usual. I also noticed a slight slurring of my speech. None of this gave me much concern. Though I was no longer a stupid teenager, I had managed to carry over a great deal of that stupidity into my 20s and decided to ignore these symptoms. I also started to notice a tingly feeling in the bottoms of my feet and toes, primarily when playing weekly pick-up basketball games. Sometimes this was accompanied by blurred vision. Again, it caused no concern. I just dealt with it by not dealing with it. The invincibility of youth still enveloped me, and I looked forward to more days of travel and adventures. Life was looking good.

LIFE HAPPENS

Today has been a rough day mentally and physically for me. I have been feeling down and out and have felt like crying for no apparent reason. I've had days like this before; they are rare though. Thank God I have an outlet to work through these emotions--my blog. I figured it was okay to share this with you all, being as you've shared my highs and lows. I pushed through and when walking, I was able to knock out 120 steps. They weren't easy, but I couldn't let up. 120 seems like I'm going backwards since 202 was my high. But I have to look at it as 120 steps is better than no steps. When I finished I had the theme song from the "Facts of Life" playing in my head.

You take the good, you take the bad,
you take them both and there you have
the facts of life, the facts of life

That's how life is, good and bad. But it's how you respond to it that matters most. Just through the course of writing this blog, my demeanor has changed from bad to good. I have a smile on my face now!

Snapping back to the harsh reality of the day-today can be jarring. I wrote this blog entry when I was discouraged. I had logged in less steps than in the previous week and it made my ultimate goal of walking again seem further away.

It makes me think of something former NY Jets Quarterback, Chad Pennington, said: "How do you look at adversity? Do you look at it as defeat or another opportunity?"

When I lay them both side by side, defeat or opportunity, the choice is clear. I don't feel defeated. I look at what I've been through, what I'm still going through, as a chance to do more. To prove my worth. To prove to myself that I've got the internal fortitude. To prove that I can both overcome adversity myself and help others overcome. This gives me renewed strength to venture forward, regardless of how many steps.

Father's Day came and went in 2001 and everything was business as usual. For me, Father's Day is now a bittersweet time of celebration at most. Of course, I think about and cherish memories I had with my dad on this day, like everyone else. I can't help but feel like an outsider, looking in, though. I don't begrudge seeing others taking their dads out to dinner and buying them unneeded but heartfelt tokens of appreciation. I took these traditions for granted for many years, but now just wish I could be the one to pick up the tab again or present the "world's best dad" mug. They say you never appreciate what you have until it's gone, but I think on Father's Day we are at least trying.

Shortly after Father's Day, on Friday, July 13th, 2001, I received a call from my mom. I was at work and my sister had stopped by. We were expecting to hear news from the doctors about our dad. He had been suffering from a constant nagging cough for several weeks until his constant nagging wife prevailed upon him to get it checked out. The news came like a ton of bricks: my father was diagnosed with terminal small-cell carcinoma. In layman's terms: lung cancer. He was given six months to live. I don't remember much after hearing that, but my sister tells me that my whole demeanor changed. She has never forgotten what I said next, "I'm too young to lose my father."

My dad was a quiet man but had quite a bit of physical presence: tall, rugged, intimidating at first glance. My friends, in fact, referred to him as John Wayne because of the smooth confidence and tough grit he projected. I can think of many examples of this, but the one that seemed to impress my friends was the lawn mower incident. My dad had been riding the mower when the front tire went flat. He turned the motor off, bent down, and, with one hand, hefted the tractor up off the ground. With his other hand, he gave a quick jerk to the tire and yanked it off, unaware of the awestruck teenage boy audience hanging off his every move.

Mom left the heavy-duty disciplining up to dad. I don't ever remember him spanking me, but his silent disappointment often left me feeling like I'd been beaten up and proved the best deterrent to foolish behavior. He was cool like that. Gentle, but authoritative. Supportive, but stern. It seemed impossible and surreal that someone so powerful could be felled by a cancer that called itself small-celled.

How do you process news like this? Anger seemed to be my most readily accessible emotion. Since I couldn't justify staying angry at my father in his state of suffering, my heavenly Father became the target of my anger. I was furious with God. I had been brought up to believe that God rewards faithfulness. Indeed, my family was incredibly faithful: church every Sunday, tithe-paying, volunteering in various areas of ministry. It now appeared that this faithfulness was not only going unrewarded, but was actually compensated with tragedy. I began to doubt the very existence of God.

Psychologists break down grieving into stages, and maybe there is some level of comfort to be had in pigeon-holing complex emotions. To say I was in

19

the anger stage oversimplifies it. I was an emotional wreck: angry, doubtful, frustrated, depressed, despairing all at once. Like many who are hurting, I fed on this emotional stew over and over again in a vain attempt to understand what was happening to me.

After a while of this, I asked myself, "Am I going to forsake everything I was raised to believe in an instant?" The answer was, "No!" I started to read books and reevaluate my faith. I concluded that the way I had lived my life up to his point had not been in vain.

My dad started receiving chemo treatments, and almost always came in to work directly from the hospital. He was often quite sick on these days and would have to lean against a pillar to catch his breath or run to the bathroom. He refused to let it get the best of him, setting a great example for me on how to live a determined life. I didn't realize how soon this lesson would come into play.

Around Christmastime of 2001, we received exciting news: the cancer was gone! This was it, the miracle we had prayed for, our faithfulness being rewarded. How glad I was that I had chosen to not abandon my faith. This news fit my paradigms about how God worked and about what was fair and right. I was relieved and elated and felt that we had been given a second lease on life.

It turned out to be a short-term lease. The cancer returned a few months later with a vengeance as did the chemo treatments. I took the cue from my dad and refused to give up hope that he would recover. I prayed more fervently than ever before. I fasted. I studied accounts of healing in the Bible. I did a ton of reading and research on faith, subconsciously thinking that if somehow I could increase and improve my flawed faith, it would make everything OK.

The last week of his life was tough. He spent a week in the hospital but was given permission to come home Father's Day weekend. Before leaving the hospital, I asked him when he was going to beat this.

He said "I haven't heard from the big guy yet."

Over the weekend, the whole family gathered around him. Comfort food abounded. We ate so much. I'm not sure why food is so tied in to loss. Maybe because eating is such an elemental activity of life and it affirms our connection to the living. I won't over-analyze, though. I like food.

Before my dad's death, there were a few scares. He was on oxygen and a few times started choking. I would run towards him to try and help, not sure if those were his last breaths. Father's Day met with a few more choking bouts. Dad also came up with some very odd questions throughout the day, a sure sign he wasn't far from death. Once he asked me if I spoke French?

I said "No, I speak Spanish. Do I need to speak French?"

He said, "No."

The other was an out-of-the blue work question. Our family business was in railroad supplies and his question was about a specific product.

"Alco 16's?" he asked.

"Shipping Monday," was my simple reply. It seemed to soothe his curiosity.

My mom stayed up with dad into the early morning of June 17th. Throughout the night, he slept fitfully, complaining of the heat, and began removing his clothing little by little. The last thing he removed was his watch, as if to say, I won't be bound by this anymore. My mom prayed a prayer of release before she drifted off to sleep. Dad died around 4 a.m.

Mom woke up shortly after and realized Dad was gone. She ran to my room, in hysterics, screaming, "He's dead, he's dead, he's dead!" and did a flying leap on top of me in my bed. Later we joked about her amateur-wrestling-inspired belly flop, but we were all too stunned by his loss to see any humor in it at the time. I called my sister a short while later. I could not bring myself to enter the room he had died in nor to look at him.

The day of the funeral came and I had prepared something to say at the services. When the time came, I just couldn't do it. This book is another way to say some of the things that were too difficult to say at the time, to say goodbye. I hope you're proud of me, Dad.

After the service, everyone was heading back to our house and a large group of cars followed behind me. I didn't really know my way home from the church and probably couldn't have focused on driving even if I did. I detoured the procession down a long gravel-road 20 minutes out of the way before we made it safely home. I kept turning down unfamiliar streets, hoping I would recognize something, but the landscape seemed alien. Eventually the last road left was the road home, which was fitting.

After my father's death came my downward spiral, physically and emotionally. Although I had recently reaffirmed my faith in God, I just truly didn't know how to handle the pain. It sounds cliché to say I turned to alcohol, but I did. Drinking wasn't a new experience for me; I had partied in high-school and occasionally got "wasted" when I went out. But now it became a problem. It's not an exaggeration to say I got drunk every night of the week. I would hide the bottles from my mom under the bed. In reality, I was hiding my anger, hurt, and pain in the temporary mental numbness that alcohol provides. I'm not proud of this, but I no longer have any reason to hide it. It was a very real part of my journey for a long time and another hurdle I would have to learn to face and overcome.

THE COLONEL

The numbness moved from my feet up to my knees. This got my attention. I finally got scared and went to the doctor. What if it traveled upwards to my heart? This was the beginning of an ongoing cycle of medical investigation into my condition: opinions and second opinions, specialists, theories, conjecture, research, all of which would continue for several years.

The first place I went was to a chiropractor. He took x-rays and performed a generalist exam. He determined it was more than a back problem and recommended I see a medical doctor. My family doctor determined it was something neurological and recommended a specialist. The specialist determined it was just a virus that would work its way out. He put me on medication, but I saw no results. I swore off doctors for awhile in frustration.

Around this time I started to have some difficulty walking—nothing too major, but I had to think about every step I took. I decided it was time to head back to the family doctor. This time he took a little more time assessing my case. In our conversation I mentioned the African gentleman who had suggested that my symptoms sounded like African Sleeping Sickness (which I'll abbreviate to ASS just to make you squirm). Curious, he busted out a medical journal to look it up. I really didn't think ASS was a real disease. I mean, doesn't it sound like something made up to scare American travelers? But it was real, and my symptoms matched quite a few of those in the journal. The journal said to call the Centers for Disease Control for treatment. Without hesitation, he called the CDC to find out what to do. They informed him of the tests to confirm a patient has ASS. Our best test option was a spinal tap, not a prospect I relished.

I scheduled an appointment for a spinal tap consult with a neurologist, an older, more 'seasoned' gentleman. Indeed, at a first glance of him, I could swear he was Colonel Sanders of Kentucky Fried Chicken fame. Heck, at 2nd and 3rd glance, too. He was the spitting and finger-licking image of his chickenly counterpart. It's a little hard to focus on a serious medical interview when you're constantly thinking in terms of "original recipe" vs. "extra crispy." To this day, I still call him "the Colonel."

At the end of the appointment, he requested I get an MRI of my brain. He told me what this entailed and I immediately started to hyperventilate. Allow me to introduce you to another of my hang-ups: I am extremely claustrophobic. The thought of lying down in a very small tube for an hour or so didn't sit well with me. He recommended an open MRI as a more appropriate option for patients like me. As it turned out, the MRI was not that bad. It was open on all sides, except for a flat rectangular apparatus I had to lie under. Other than being slightly conscious of how similar this might be to a chicken breast lying under one of the Colonel's heat lamps, I hardly felt any claustrophobic anxiety. The spinal tap was administered as an outpatient procedure at the local hospital. Colonel Doctor entered the room with his implements of torture in hand. He talked me through what was going to happen, but all I heard were panic phrases like "gigantic needle" and "stabbing pain." He started with multiple shots around my back, numbing up the area around my spine. He then attempted to insert the needle. Once. Twice. Third time was the charm.

The moment the needle entered my spine, I immediately broke out into a horrible sweat and nearly passed out. Once I got my bearings and started to feel better, he let me know that if he hadn't succeeded that third time, he would have had to get the BIG needle out. Now I don't know about you, but I pictured an extraordinarily large needle you might see a cartoon doctor use. Wow, I dodged a bullet there. That was the worst pain I had ever felt in my life. If you can avoid getting a spinal tap it would be a wise choice.

Since walking was becoming increasingly difficult, I had high hopes that these two tests would reveal the cause of my declining health and it could be speedily rectified. This hope was met by waiting and more waiting. This waiting on test results was a new experience for me, but one which would become all too familiar over the years.

My mom and I finally sat down with the Colonel to hear his diagnosis. He saw nothing too alarming or significant from either procedure, and threw out the term "transverse myelitis." I had enough of the symptoms he described to make me think this might be what I had.

Colonel Doctor gave me a prescription similar to the one the last neurologist had given me. I wasn't too thrilled with that, but he's the doctor, so I followed his instruction. In the meantime, I had an eye appointment. After the MRI and spinal tap, this round of testing was a breath of fresh air. The eye doctor reported definite vision problems. He inquired about my health issues and I informed him of what I knew to date. He was confident that what I was battling could not be transverse myelitis and he asked for Colonel Doctor's contact info so he could write him a letter about this. I happily obliged and left his office feeling like I had found an advocate for my case.

In my next meeting with Colonel Doctor, he

expressed some doubt around his diagnosis of TM and spoke of looking deeper into my condition. Since it was the eye doctor who first pointed this out, I left the meeting once again disillusioned with all doctors. I didn't know what my next move should be, so I took another hiatus. During this time off from doctors, a good friend introduced me to a doctor he knew from Africa. She recommended a consult with an expert on infectious diseases and hooked me up with a university specialist. I made an exception and scheduled an appointment. I told this latest doctor about my trip to Africa and my subsequent medical history. He began his typical neurological exam by removing my shoes and socks for some tests. He noticed my webbed toes. I told him that when I got back from Africa a couple of my toes on each foot became webbed. He looked up at me puzzled for a moment before I told him I was joking; I was born like that. We got a good laugh out of that.

I tend to make corny jokes when I'm in uncomfortable situations. Who am I kidding? I tell corny jokes all the time. At any rate, he finished up and gave a diagnosis that was just as laughable as my webbed toe stunt.

He said, "It sounds like just a case of bad jet lag." I naturally thought he was joking, but quickly realized he was dead serious. "Are you kidding me?" I thought. That Africa trip was three years ago and I've been steadily getting worse since. I was frustrated, confused, angry. Not being a fan of conflict or uneasy situations, I took the news calmly and went on my way.

On the road home, I thought long and hard about my situation. What should I do now? My health was getting worse. The numbness in my legs had reached my waist and I didn't know when or where it would stop. Imagine how your foot or hand feels when it falls asleep and you'll get a sense for how it felt, only I never could manage to wake them up. The numbness was constant and on the move and this scared me.

I knew I needed a break from the frustration of dealing with all of these doctors and the uncertainty of a diagnosis. And that's what I did. I took my break and just lived my life.

Detour

Even though the two trips I had taken to Mexico and Africa weren't the smoothest of trips for me, I still wanted to travel. The appeal of visiting new places and having new experiences far outweighed the negatives I had endured on previous trips. My friend Carmen had been living in Germany for a year or so when my buddy Bob and I planned a trip to visit her. The three of us had previously travelled to the Salt Lake Olympics together and had wanted to do a more ambitious trip.

This trip would be great for me mentally. I could leave behind the increasing frustrations of my health problems and brooding over the approaching anniversary of my dad's death, and just relax for a change. This was no mission trip, but a real vacation, and I drooled in anticipation at all the new experiences awaiting.

Bob and I booked a flight with a connection in Philadelphia. We continued on to Munich, Germany, and I took some comfort in how travel-savvy I was becoming. Flying over the ocean this time? No big deal.

As we elbowed our way out past customs, Carmen welcomed us with open arms, beaming, so happy to see familiar faces from the states. We were equally pleased to see her. She offered us the option to relax in Germany for the day or to hit the ground running. We opted to hit the road, destination--Italy. We headed for Vicenza, grateful that Carm had shipped her trusty sedan over from the states and was more than comfortable driving on the Autobahn. Since Carmen worked on contract for the United States military, we took advantage of her military discount by staying on bases along the way. We grabbed some dinner at a local eatery, which was fabulous, probably more so since we were in friggin' Italy.

For breakfast, oddly enough, we made our way to an on-base American staple fast food joint and downed our sandwiches, fortified for our train ride into Venice. Along the way, we met some American soldiers and our lively conversations with them made the time pass much more quickly.

Ah, Venice. What a site! An entire city on water, so much to take in. I'll never forget San Marco's square, home to the largest dance floor in the world and what must be the world's greatest concentration of pigeons. They were everywhere, lounging about, socializing, running their little pigeon errands, jaded to the taunting of children. Like paparazzi, tourists young and old were busily snapping pictures, in awe of their sheer numbers. Bob was quick to discover that they were tame or dumb enough to perch on his arm and insisted we make the most of this golden photo opp. Carmen and I were less enthusiastic about this invasion of our personal space, but we eventually relented. Bob snapped a picture of me looking rather skittish at the "rat with wings" crawling up my arm.

After that adventure, we boarded a water taxi to the island of Murano where the famous Murano glass is made. We got a tour of the facility and a glass blowing demonstration and left laden with glass souvenirs.

No account of our Tour d'Italy is complete without a nod to gelato. Now I love good homemade ice cream, but I got my first taste of gelato in Venice. What a creamy delight--so smooth, so many flavors, so many gelato shops, so little time. It seemed like we stopped at every gelato establishment we came to, not that I'm complaining. We couldn't get enough of the stuff.

As sunset approached that first day, we found ourselves at a place where the city appeared to end abruptly, just some steps leading down directly into the sea. We sat there, watching the sun go down and recounting the events of the day. Somehow, our conversation meandered to events of my life over the last couple of years. I will never forget what we talked about next. Over the last few years, I had been afraid to get too close to anyone and consider them a friend. I'm not really sure if that was my fear of getting close to someone and then losing them as I had my father or what. But this night was different and I realized that friendships are a wonderful thing. To have people you can count on and that are there for you no matter what is nothing short of amazing. I've never felt that more keenly than on those steps at the end of the world.   To this day, I still get a little emotional thinking about that night.   I'm glad I opened myself up to care for people and to be cared for.

Part of me--probably the get-to-the-point, bottom-line business side of my brain--wants to skip relating details of the visit to Europe. I also realize that there are life lessons to be learned at all points of the journey, even in the detours.   That which changes our course is also a chance to take a 'scenic route' and discover new things.

Detours are a part of life, whether by choice or chance. Since we're here, we might as well relax and open ourselves up. Open our eyes to see the beauty around us. Open our ears to hear what the world is saying.   Open our hearts to be truly moved.

It was difficult to say good bye to Venice. Cinque

Terre helped soften the blow, five little villages which are built into the rocks of the coastline, nestled picturesquely between the beach and gently terraced hills and vineyards of Tuscany.

Although it had just been a couple of days away, I found myself missing friends, family and the simple conveniences of home. When we first arrived in Cinque Terre, I carved out some alone time just to call home to hear some familiar voices. Amazingly, this simple time-out helped me get over my momentary home-sickness. It reminds me of one of my voice recordings from 2006:

> I was just thinking about missing the little things, like being able to stand up to take a shower. Being able to stand in front of a mirror and do my hair or put in contacts. Being able to stand up and pick my clothes and get dressed. Putting on a belt or kneeling down to tie my shoes. Being able to stand up and cook dinner. There are a lot of things I can do from a wheelchair. I get excited when I can manage to cook something from the chair. A part of me wants to cry for the loss of these things. Being able to jump into my car and drive somewhere, crank the music and just go. No matter where: work, church, to grab a soda, anywhere. In missing these small things I've realized that each step of the process has brought something new or different. Having to deal with many set-backs and work-arounds has truly given me an appreciation for the little things, often so

simple and seemingly inconsequential, but just what the doctor ordered.

Cinque Terre is best reached by boat, and what a beautiful day that was for a boat ride. We soon shimmied up to the docking area. I use the term "docking area" loosely. It was more like, "let's find a random spot to tie the boat off, lower the plank, and dump out the passengers onto the rocks below." I know it sounds like pirates were involved, but maybe that's just me. Since the five villages are situated in the cliffs, we had to climb up seemingly endless stone steps to get to the first village. But what a cool payoff. The village was San Francisco-like with its streets, uphill one way and downhill the other. Quaint shops and eateries comingled cozily with the residential cottages.

In between the villages, lurked a narrow, sloping pathway to the next town. My vertigo kicked in big time at first glance of this. The path overlooked the sea and jagged rocks below. My knees trembled; my stomach churned; my brain refused to relay messages to my feet to proceed forward. We were forced to find an alternate route for me and discovered, to my relief, a small rail service also provided passage between towns. Ever the adventurous ones, Bob and Carmen left me to wait for the train and hiked up the connecting path. I guess in a way I felt adventurous, too: on my own in a foreign country, taking the train myself. Such a big boy. At least that was my way of looking at it.

Out of the corner of my eye, I noticed a lady approaching me.

"Great," I thought. "I'm going to have to use the little bit of Spanish I know (it's as close to Italian as I can get) to tell her I don't speak Italian."

To my amazement, a distinctly Bostonian-accented voice asked if I knew the time. We struck up a conversation that continued on the train ride. God always knows just what we need when we need it. That lady helped put me at ease after the stress of not being able to conquer my fear of heights and being on my own in the CT.

I soon reunited with my friends and we explored the towns for awhile until dinner. We found a delightful outdoor restaurant with a gorgeous view. Wow, breathtaking! I'm not sure if it was the view that made our dinner taste so good, but that was definitely the best pesto I've ever had.

The theme song for the next segment of the trip was the B-52's hit, *Roam*. I think I looked most forward to visiting Rome than any other place. Just to see the Coliseum would be enough for me, but I discovered that Rome had much more to offer. Getting there in one piece was another story.

Romans are among the scariest drivers I've ever seen. Racing down Chicago's expressways was nothing new to me, but in Rome, I feared for my life. Thankfully, no accidents occurred and we arrived safely.

On our way to see the Coliseum, we got sidetracked by a venue near the ruins of the Roman Senate that looked decked out to host a concert of some sort. Carmen, the member of our trio most susceptible to wanderlust, noticed a gap in the fenced off area and egged us on to sneak in. Bob hesitantly followed, but being the resident wuss of the group, I stayed back. They trespassed toward the tower of an ancient ruin shrouded in scaffolding. Before I knew it, Carmen was scaling the scaffolding while Bob tried in vain to talk her down off that ledge. Eventually, she relented and came down.

Once they squeezed back through the gate, though, an angry Italian woman lay in wait. Boy did she let them have it. I had naturally shied away and tried to blend in with some other tourists, but even from that distance I could tell the woman was furious. At the conclusion of her tirade, which distinctly included the word 'polizia' several times, Carmen and Bob shrugged ignorantly, and said, "English?" I doubt if this helped their cause. We high-tailed it out of there when the agitated matron stopped to catch her breath.

We forged ahead to the Coliseum but not before ducking into a bistro across the street. What a beautiful backdrop for a quick bite. We arrived a bit too late for the daily inside tours of the Coliseum, but I really didn't care. I was only too thrilled to be in such a historical place.

We also checked out the Trevi fountain, the Spanish Steps and other typical tourist sites. As the day came to a close, we made our way to the subway. Big mistake, at least as far as I was concerned. The way out to street level involved a trek up the tallest, steepest escalator I have ever seen. Talk about facing my fear. When I looked up, I could barely make out where the end was. Too late to turn back, I swallowed hard, held my breath, lowered my head down and held on for dear life. I made it fine, but I definitely wouldn't take the subway again.

The next day's plan included a trip to the Vatican. While figuring out our next steps, we inadvertently latched in to a tour with a guide named Anna. The tour was free, at least for the first hour. She took us through St. Peter's Basilica pointing out and explaining all of the statues and such.

The second part of the tour, which included the Sistine Chapel, required a hefty fee, but we gladly paid and Anna's professionalism and expertise were well worth it. Also since I shamelessly flirted with Anna the whole time, she made me stand behind a headless statue so the whole group could take funny pictures. We were close that way. The tour ended at the Sistine Chapel. We were continuously shushed by the guards and couldn't take pictures, but the artwork was truly awe-inspiring.

That evening, Bob and Carmen wanted to check out a few more sites and had their eyes set on a certain restaurant. I decided to head back to the hotel since my legs were starting to give out. We had walked around a ton and the fatigue really hit me harder than normal. Back at the hotel I hunkered down for the evening with some DVDs, only venturing out to a local panini shop when my stomach serenaded me with an ode to hunger. Florence awaited us the next day.

Soon, like Willie Nelson, we were "on the road again." We made a bee-line for the Galleria dell'Accademia to ogle the Statue of David. I was surprised at how big it was. (I'm talking about the *entire* statue, of course.) Overall, Florence struck me as quite an artist's haven, with plenty of great architecture and history to explore.

We got somewhat carried away in Florence and realized as we arrived at our military base lodging that we had forgotten to eat (besides some gelato earlier in the day of course). We drove around looking for a repast, but to no avail. Back at the barracks, we were greeted by a beacon of light calling to us: two vending machines shining brightly in the darkness. Mountain Dew and Cheetos sufficed as the dinner of choice for three weary travelers that night.

The next day, we planned on a day of fun in the sun at the "American Beach," so named because the military types frequented it. Luckily for us, we pretty much had the entire beach to ourselves. We set up on the beach and ordered silly drinks. Boy, what a way to spend the day after being on the go non-stop since we stepped off the plane in Germany. And a gorgeous day it was! The glistening water lovingly whispered our names, and unable to resist her siren call, we plunged in for a dip. Ahhh, refreshing! How nice it was to be swimming in the Mediterranean Sea in friggin' Italy.

We spent the full day there, lounging in the sun. In hindsight, maybe that wasn't such a great idea without sunscreen. Carmen had slathered herself with it, but Bob and I were too macho to bother with that (and would pay for it later). That night we found a nice little rustic Italian restaurant for dinner. The dessert course was quite memorable and Carmen's was the most interesting; it came to the table flaming. The flames were so high that putting the fire out was a challenge that took the efforts and ingenuity of all three of us. We finally doused it, only to discover that the wad of gelato underneath was totally melted. I mean, who came up with the idea of flaming gelato? What a waste!

Tomorrow's journey would bring us to Pisa, so we settled down early. I tossed and turned all night. I'd like to say it was due to the excitement of getting to see the Leaning Tower the next day, but the truth is that my over-cooked and crispy skin kept me up. Showering and dressing were quite painful. Bob was in the same predicament and we each spent the next few days trying to inflict stealthy back slaps on each other just to rub it in, so to speak.

It was pretty cool being on location in front of the famed and oft-photographed Leaning Tower of Pisa, but I have to say it was pretty much in the middle of nowhere. That gelato stand across the street had my name on it, though. Naturally we had to identify ourselves as American tourists and do the classic "holding-up-the-Tower" pose. This was our last stop before heading back to Germany.

This part of the journey was a bit too roller coaster-like for my comfort: up into and down from the seemingly endless mountains. At one point, I had to close my eyes and crank up my MP3 player. A few words with the "Man upstairs" sure helped, too.

In Germany once again, Carmen and Bob decided to take a detour to hike up to this famous old castle. Of course, being polite, they asked if I wanted to hike with them. No way was I going to hike up there. I just stayed back in the car watching my DVDs on my laptop.

Darkness was settling in as we pulled in to Amberg, Germany, where Carmen lived. Carmen asked us if we wanted to go to Prague the next day. It was a tempting offer, but we opted out. A nice relaxing day at Carmen's house was just what we needed for our last day before returning to the States.

Waking up on our last full day on vacation was bittersweet. It would be nice to get back home; at the same time it had been wonderful to hang with Carmen and to get away from all the day-to-days. We planned on a back-porch barbeque that afternoon, so Carmen escorted us to the town square to get some baked goodies for breakfast and farmer's market food for the grill. While munching on our authentic Bavarian pretzels, I was shocked to see how many of the Ambergers were drinking beer at 10 o'clock in the morning.

We recounted our adventures while grilling out. It had been such a fantastic time and we were sad to see it coming to an end. Although I was ready for the comforts of home, I wasn't quite ready to deal with my health issues again.

Steroids and Herbs

By the spring of 2004, my health had continued to decline, though it seemingly took a holiday at certain points of its travel through my body. I started to notice the numbness on the move again, impairing my ability to walk even further. I had arrived at another crossroads. Why couldn't life be Italy all the time--free of stress and big decisions? The biggest decision I had to worry about over there was what flavor of gelato to get. I truly did not feel prepared for what lay ahead. I dreaded more doctor appointments, but what other choice did I have?

While I was still in limbo on what to do next, my sister had learned that a friend of a friend had some similar ailments. A neurosurgeon discovered a blood clot on this person's brain. They operated and the symptoms evaporated. So I jumped right on board and was able to schedule an appointment with the same doctor. I was so excited, thinking naively that my problems would easily be solved. The weeks leading up to the appointment dragged on. During this period I researched brain surgery to see what it would entail. I felt like I should be prepared. What I found was not exactly encouraging. I would need to be awake while they drilled through my skull. Eventually, I came to grips with this possibility. If that's what I have to endure to get better, it would be a small price to pay.

Finally, the day arrived. I was nervous, but mostly excited. Arms laden with stacks of prior test results, my sister and I confidently made our way in to get our answer. First things first: a list of questions. They wanted as much detail as we could give, all of it helpful for the diagnosis. This idea of disclosing every detail about my health was still new to me. Blurred vision, muscle pains, bladder discomfort--all of them clues to unlocking my mystery. I'm sure I wasn't as detailed as I could've been, but it was the best I knew at the time. In the not-too-distant future, my sister would write up my complete and meticulously detailed medical history. I have to take time out to say my sister, Kim, rocks! She has been the best advocate for my situation.

After pouring through my stacks of test results and completing their neurological tests, the neurosurgeon presented his non-answer answer. The problem wasn't as simple as we had hoped. There was no easy fix like surgery (not that surgery would be a picnic, but at least it represented a finite and tangible step, one-stop shopping, if you will). I was told to see a general neurologist. I had, in fact, already seen two in recent history and wasn't looking forward to it. I reluctantly scheduled an appointment, hoping this experience would be better than the previous ones.

Two weeks flew by. In yet another waiting room, I thought to myself, "What's this guy going to tell me now? It's a virus that'll work its way out? Or probably just bad jet lag?" I had prepared myself for some such nonsense.

We spent an hour with this doctor during which he administered the typical neurological exam and interview and after which he told us to come back in a week. He would formulate a plan of attack during this time. My walking regressed even further while we waited. It was frustrating to see something I took so for granted now becoming a real challenge. It was embarrassing to stumble and fall in front of people. I know before I wasn't excited or even looking forward to seeing another neurologist, but now I was at a point where I didn't care who helped figure things out; just figure them out. I couldn't keep going down this road of declining health.

At our appointment, the doctor noticed my ability to walk had become more difficult since our last meeting. My steps were shaky and more deliberate. His plan of attack was to order me up a couple of MRI's--this time at their facility in a closed MRI. Oh joy. In about a week I would get to have the feeling of being buried alive. So far I wasn't skeptical with this doctor like I had become with the others. Maybe it was just my wanting to get to the bottom of things and get better that was causing me to be more trusting.

The moment of MRI truth had come, and I started feeling a weight on my chest and began hyperventilating. Though I was super nervous, I knew I needed to do this. "Here goes nothing," I thought.

In no time, I was back in the waiting room to meet my mom and sister. They were both amazed at how fast the procedure went. I looked down at the tile and said nothing. It was the nurse who busted me out.

"He got into the MRI and a few short minutes later we had to pull him out."

I replied, "There was no way I could've stayed in there."

The nurse said we would have to let my doctor know of my claustrophobia and make sure I get some drugs in me so I could make it through the test. Not only did I have the humbling job of telling my doctor I couldn't get through the test, but I got to deal with the ridicule of my sister the rest of the day.

Soon enough, I was back for the MRI; this time adequately drugged. Even though they fitted me with head phones set to a smooth jazz station, it wasn't enough to drown out the jackhammer noise of the MRI. That still wasn't the worst part of the test. My shoulders were jammed up against the sides of the machine until they started to burn, and I still had 20 minutes left. At about the 10 minute point, I had to have them pull me out. I couldn't take it anymore. They let me out of the coffin for a few minutes but talked me into finishing the last 10 minutes. It was rough, but I was able to walk into the waiting room and look my sister in the eyes and tell her I did it!

After looking over the test results and seeing my decline, the doctor suggested I go into the hospital for a week and receive IV steroids. I wasn't getting any better, so sure, why not? Let's get 'roided up. I was actually kind of looking forward to it.

In the hospital, I scored a single room. Sweet! I didn't think a hospital stay could get any better than this: a room all to myself, getting pumped full of drugs for one full week, and great food nearby. We pigged out at a great Italian restaurant before I checked in. The server brought out the orders to our table, asking about the fourth person in our party. Boy, did we feel fat at that moment; there were only three of us. We didn't finish all of our food that day, but I made sure I put a dent in it.

It seemed like every night someone showed up, just in time for dinner, and brought me some grub from the area. Most nights, it was from the Italian joint, but I also sampled a classic Polish from another well-known restaurant. My travel buddy Bob, even brought by some gelato, carrying me back to the great memories from Italy.

By the end of that week, my doctor had some news. After looking over my test results and seeing the progress made with the steroids, he gave me a diagnosis of MS: Multiple Sclerosis. I really wasn't sure what that meant. He shared that he was only 93% sure. I always thought doctors spoke in black and white terms, but this diagnosis seemed gray to me. Although I was not fully convinced of the diagnosis, I felt good about the improvement I had with the steroids. So I would keep seeing him.

At the end of my stay, I had a physical therapist visit my room to bring me a walker for days that I needed a little support. I took it, but my pride wasn't going to let me use it. "Only elderly people use them," I thought. In fact, by the time my stay was over, I was able to walk out of the hospital with more confidence than when I walked in. My legs felt much stronger, which seemed to have made my balance better. My doctor did warn me, however, to keep an eye out for when I started to decline again.

The decline came on more quickly than I wanted to admit. It was weeks before I informed my doctor of it, though. I even used the walker on more occasions than I would've liked. The end result was another week in the hospital for steroids. This was not ideal, but something had to be done. At least I would be close to some good food again. This time around we also scheduled an appointment with a psychiatrist. Not feeling so confident with the MS diagnosis, we thought I might be suffering from post-traumatic stress disorder brought about by my father's passing.

Sure enough, a new white coat presented himself and dug right in with the questions. It felt weird opening my life to a stranger, but I knew I needed to let myself be an open book and hopefully help get some more answers. It was kind of nice letting my emotions out to an unbiased third party. At the end of the session, I was offered an anti-depressant for a month. I figured it couldn't hurt anything, so I agreed. I saw improvement from the steroid/anti-depressant cocktail. Physically, I was stronger due to the steroids while at the same time more pleasant to be around. I guess 'roid raging really is a side effect of taking steroids in any fashion. I'm a high strung person to begin with, but being on steroids kicked it up a notch. Since I worked with my family every day, they dealt with the brunt of my anger. They were happy during the month I was on the anti-depressant.

As soon as I noticed deterioration in my walking, I became proactive and scheduled an outpatient appointment for another round of steroids. This entailed going in and being hooked up for an hour or so to an IV, but no overnight stay. I can be a bit of a control freak, in addition to being high-strung. I was starting to hate these week-long steroid treatments because it took me away from the business. I was on the phone a lot at the hospital, making sure everything was getting done. I guess my obsession was mainly because I was still trying to make my dad proud, even though he was gone.

I noticed I was becoming progressively worse as each treatment wore off. The next treatment, in fact, I showed up in a wheelchair. My walking was minimal and unsafe. After my second outpatient treatment, I was definitely stronger and able to do more walking, but staying up for an extended period of time took a lot out of me. While at work, I'd mostly get around on an electric scooter for safety's sake.

I spent a long time stewing in the waiting room at my next appointment. Some pharmaceutical reps walked out, reminding me of the discouraging research Kim and I had done on MS drugs. They won't get you better, but hopefully lengthen the time between relapses. That's not something you want to hear. There isn't a drug to get you better. I was growing more and more frustrated. A 45 minute wait didn't help matters. When I finally was called in, the doctor apologized, stating that the reps had taken him out for a lunch. "Nice," I thought. He noticed I was in the wheelchair and told me I've got to do something. "Really?" I thought to myself. That's putting it nicely. He then asked me what drug I wanted to take. There were numerous options. All I heard was "What drug do you want to take for the rest of your life and never get better?" That got me hot! My sister noticed my face turning bright red. Knowing I'm a hothead, she feared I was going to say something I'd regret. Surprisingly, I did not. I told him I have to think about it some more and I left his office.

This wouldn't do. After discussing my sentiments with my sister, I decided I wasn't ready to start taking a drug that would never get me better. She agreed. It was time to explore other options, but I needed some time to cool off first. After the cool down, Kim and I talked about numerous options, but there was one we couldn't get away from: Chinese acupuncture. I searched online and found a place not far from work that specialized in Chinese herbal medicine. That wasn't exactly what I was looking for, but perhaps they did acupuncture, too. What did I have to lose? So I gave them a call. I got right through to someone and the heavily-accented voice on the opposite end left no room for doubt that this was the real deal. I began to tell him that I was looking for a place to receive acupuncture. I wasn't really sure if he heard or understood me. He began asking a wide array of questions. I told him I had MS-like symptoms. He wanted to know more detail. So I shared: my ability to walk had grown difficult, vision was blurry, speech could be a little slurred, and the most recent development: my bladder had grown a mind of its own.

He took it all in stride and scheduled an afternoon appointment with me. His "office" address was a house about a half hour from work. I passed on the information to Kim and told her of our conversation. In our typical fashion, we had a good laugh about yet another shifty doctor, and she looked up all she could about him on the Internet. With confidence that he wasn't a total whack job, I headed out for my appointment.

My first impression was that this must be the creepy house on the block that all the kids dare each other to approach. Blinds covered all of the windows, and I couldn't detect any movement in the house. After what seemed to be 15 minutes of waiting, the door abruptly swung open. A frail, wiry Chinese man, whom we'll call Dr. Lee, invited me inside in broken English. I removed my shoes, since that seemed like the thing to do, and sat on a couch directly across from him. I cautiously scanned my surroundings. There didn't appear to be much in the house. The living room consisted of two large couches and I noticed down the hall a computer on a small desk. The pinched blinds allowed just enough sunbeams to stream through that I could see all the dust in the air, contributing to the overall creepy factor. Nevertheless, I wasn't really concerned for my safety. He was five foot nothing and a hundred and nothing. I was pretty sure I could take him if need be.

He grilled me with a list of questions. Even though I had been through this many times before, I found myself second guessing some of my answers. Suddenly, he moved next to me and began checking my pulse. He then asked me to stick out my tongue. I thought he was going to look at my tonsils, so I stuck out my tongue and went AHHHHHHHHHHHH. Little did I know he just wanted to look at my tongue. Apparently in Chinese medicine, you can tell a lot about the body just by looking at a person's tongue. He jotted down some cryptic notes and then handed me a Ziploc baggie filled with a brown powder. I was thinking, "Whoa, is this a drug deal going down?" It kind of felt like that. He then asked for my check.

He instructed me how to take the herbs. He only gave me one week's worth to make sure my body could handle them. I was to split the baggie into 14 equal parts and take a dose once in the morning and once at night. It required stirring the herbs in hot water and drinking the mixture down. After my first sampling, I was sure this wasn't a drug deal. The herbs did not bring me into a state of euphoria or well-being or funky hallucinations. They tasted like dirt.

My diet needed to change also to a mix of 30% meat and 70% vegetables. I was told to drink only hot water—never cold. Alcohol and cigarettes were absolutely off limits. Without hesitation, I agreed and stopped both immediately. I'm not sure why it was so easy to give those up but I thank God it was. Also during this week I was to keep an eye out for a rash. If a rash occurred I was to stop the herbs immediately. Armed with the information and my herbs, I ventured out to test out this new lifestyle.

I had been on the Atkins diet the past month, so I had plenty of meat, but outside of iceberg lettuce, no vegetables graced my crisper. A trip to the grocery store was in my future, but I had to figure out first what I could actually eat and prepare. Internet to the rescue to find some good recipes. But did I mention that I wasn't allowed any outside seasonings either? Dr. Lee had put it this way: if a corporation makes it, it's no good. Was he crazy?

As with most new diets for me, the first few days were the easiest. The biggest challenge was choking down those herbs after each breakfast and dinner. I swear it was like ground up sod in hot water. Without fail, there were always some herbal dregs at the bottom of the cup that I had to spoon feed myself. Dr. Lee's commandment was to get every last bit. Mmmm. Bad to the last drop.

After six days of the treatments, I had a follow-up call with Dr. Lee. Before the call I thought I'd better check for that rash. Sure enough, an ugly red blotch stained my forearm. I debated telling the doctor because I was afraid he'd tell me that herbs wouldn't work, and frankly, I was holding out a lot of hope that this would cure me once and for all. I knew I had to report it, though.

I outed myself on the rash and to my relief, Dr. Lee said he would simply adjust the herb dosage. I always stress about things and usually find out it isn't necessary.

Dr. Lee doled out the new and improved batch of herbs. "God," I prayed, "Please let these work." I knew these herbs were different, but they sure looked the same appetizing dirt brown color as before. Eureka, a week went by with no rash! Since all went well that week, he gave me two week's worth next at a significant cost savings. I noticed a weird sensation in my ankles during those two weeks. It felt good, considering I'd had little to no feeling from my waist down to my toes for some time. I also began to lose weight, no doubt an outcome of the diet change.

The *gain* of losing weight and getting some sensation back was offset by a couple of negatives. First, my ability to walk had become basically nonexistent. The scooter I was using at work now became my legs at home. Second, I could no longer control my bladder. I had always thought of adult diapers as a product for old people, but I was learning how wrong I was. I would try to make it to the bathroom in time, but usually failed. One day, in fact, I got to the bathroom, wiggled off of my scooter and onto the toilet only to realize I had transferred too aggressively. I actually broke the toilet! Water was pouring out. The rest was a blur, but somehow I managed to hoist myself back on to the scooter and rushed over to my sister's office. Once the situation was under control, all we could do was laugh and then brainstorm an alternative way to combat my willful bladder.

We eventually found a website that specialized in external catheters. Basically a condom-like cup fits around the penis with a hose attached to the bottom that runs along your leg down to a bag. Wasn't ideal, but it got the job done.

One big lesson I was learning through this: when things in life don't go the way you've planned, make a new plan. You have to adapt. The main adaptation needs to occur within YOU, but people that love you have to adapt too. For many, it can be very difficult to see a family member or friend healthy and full of life one moment and disabled the next. Don't be discouraged if that's the case. Keeping your attitude positive is what will help them overcome the difficulty of seeing you in such a shape.

A New Friend

In September of 2005, my second cousin was turning three. I always went to her birthday parties. Even with things so difficult for me, I was determined to get there. I was hopeful I could navigate the party on my scooter. When I arrived, several family members helped me walk into the house. That's the last time I remember walking.

I knew it was going to be a good day because the Bears had won another game. After the game, I got on my "ride" and tore my way over to a group of friends, among them, an old high school chum, Heather. I struck up a conversation with her.

She asked, "What's with the scooter?"

Knowing she was unaware of my situation, I teased a bit and said, "I'm just lazy." I then proceeded to tell her my story. I could see in her eyes she felt bad once I told her the truth. I didn't mean to make her feel bad.

Heather had brought a friend with her to the party. The three of us sat around the table just talking. They were very interested in finding out what was up with me. So I shared. Since I was having a "bad eye day," (yes, there are worse things than bad hair) I wasn't able to focus too sharply. But Heather's friend made an impression. I could tell that she had curly hair and she was a real good listener, or at least a good pretender. And she seemed very nice. We were interrupted by the serving of the birthday cake and opening of gifts, and soon afterward Heather and her curly-haired friend said their goodbyes. I decided it was time for me to leave too. Thinking about driving home kind of worried me though. My vision was blurry and I felt kind of weak. I debated giving it a try, but decided to play it safe and called my sister. She and her fiancé, Joe, offered to take me home.

I'll never forget that day—a day of lasts. Last time I walked, last time I drove. The progression was tough. The day I knew I couldn't drive without some assistance was bad enough. But then, I got hand controls and safely maneuvered around with those for over a year. This latest development meant that I possibly would never drive again. Period. I don't like to say never. Just as I knew I'd walk again, I felt confident in the fact that I'd drive again.

Back at the home front, I had nothing more to do than partake in a favorite mindless pastime: surfing the web. I had set up a web site with a guest book and had numerous friends signing it and leaving nice comments. Are you kidding me? Heather's friend, Emily as it turned out, left me a comment. She wrote about how it was nice to meet me and talk to someone so positive about life. She beat me to the punch. I was going to e-mail Heather, asking for her information. This made things easier. I responded immediately to thank her for her nice words. I hoped we could start a communication, maybe even get to see her again.

I invited her over the next Sunday. The occasion, I told her, was football day. She was fine with that. My nervous level shot up. She arrived well after kick-off. She took a seat comfortably next to me on the couch. We chatted briefly about how we knew Heather before getting down to the business of getting to know each other. We talked for hours. It was well into the evening before we said our goodbyes. We would definitely be in touch again.

I really liked this girl. I started spending all my free time texting and e-mailing her. I think my dad was right. He always said, "When a boy's girling, he ain't worth two cents." I miss him like crazy, but remembering things he said helps me feel just a little closer to him. So, he's still around. And he would have said I was girling. Hard.

One day, I asked Emily if she wanted to join me at a lunch with my family. It was my sister Kim's birthday, so Kim, Joe, my mom, and her boyfriend would be coming over. She told me that she was nervous about that.

So I said to her, "What, you've never met the family of a friend before?"

There was silence and then she let me know she wouldn't be able to stay after all. She left fairly abruptly after that. My statement had upset her. I really didn't think it was that big of a deal.

At lunch, my sister asked where Emily was. I told her that she would not be coming. Knowing me all too well and figuring I had screwed something up, she asked, "What did you do now?"

I told her what I had said and how that seemed to upset Emily. She told me how stupid that was of me. Leave it to my sister to tell me the truth. Emily was more than just a friend to me and I knew that. Once again I had let my own stupidity rule the day, but Kim saw through this and helped me realize how much I really did care for her. Thankfully Emily didn't stay too mad at me, and she agreed to come over later that day. I guess she was showing me forgiveness.

What an idiot! Even with this cloud of illness over me, I needed to get my head straight if this relationship was going to work. I never expected that things would progress so quickly between me and Emily. I guess the lesson I learned from my detour in Italy was serving me well right now: keep yourself open. I kept my heart open and Emily found her way in.

As I thought more and more about me and Emily, feelings surfaced that I had never felt before, and I wasn't quite sure how to put them into words. I soon figured it out. One December evening, on my birthday in fact, with Emily next to me on the couch, the emotions bubbled over and I said to her, "I love you!"

With that utterance came a rush of nervousness and excitement. Oh my gosh! What a feeling to share my love and for it to be received and reciprocated. I had great hope that this good feeling would carry over into my physical recovery.

One day, Dr. Lee broached the idea of combining acupuncture with the herbs, explaining that the two treatments complimented each other. He recommended only one doctor he trusted to work with me. Again, I was willing to give anything a shot and set up a series of appointments.

My first appointment was acupuncture and chiropractic. Not as bad as I had expected for a treatment that involves having numerous thin needles driven into various spots on my body. The scalp needle felt the strangest. Threading the scalp with a thin needle was weird, not painful, just odd. Despite the weirdness of the treatments, I found the sitting in the dark for 15 minutes during treatments very relaxing. I normally don't allow myself the time to just rest and reflect.

At our next appointment, she ran some tests, including several outside-the-box tests, one of which was a screening for Lyme disease. I'd been tested for this before, but hers wasn't the standard FDA-approved test. Why not go for it, since I was pursuing an alternate route anyway? As we waited for the test results, I continued to notice slight improvements with Chinese herbs and acupuncture. I felt sensations in my lower legs, definitely a welcome sign. Also, since starting acupuncture, color had returned to my otherwise white and lifeless feet.

After only my second week of acupuncture and first month of herbs, I grew tired of the slight steps toward healing. It sounds ridiculous, but I had wanted to be up and walking at this point, even though I understood that it had taken a long time for me to regress physically.

Dr. Pierce, the acupuncture doctor, asked to meet with me before my third treatment. She wanted Kim to be in the room with me. She wasted no time once we were assembled. "The test results are back," she stated. "You have Lyme disease." I felt a rush of emotions. To finally have a diagnosis nearly brought me to tears. I think Kim was nearly there too, but her logical brain kicked in and she asked, "What's next?"

Dr. Pierce recommended a treatment center in Kansas City, where she knew a doctor that had successfully diagnosed and treated several Lyme patients. She put us in contact both with the doctor and a recent patient of his.

I left there on a high. I can't express how exciting it was to finally have a diagnosis. I shared the news with family and friends via cell phone on the way home. I couldn't wait to tell Emily. Finally there seemed to be light at the end of the tunnel.

As usual, the light flickered a bit and at times seemed to disappear entirely. I finally got through to a representative only to learn that the earliest available slot for treatment was for March of 2006--roughly four months away. Left with no other option, I dejectedly scheduled the appointment.

Thankfully, Dr. Pierce commiserated with my predicament and contacted a board-certified doctor at her facility. She was able to get me a consultation which led to a script for an oral medication. Dr. Lee wasn't crazy about the idea, but relented, so I was approved. By then it was Christmastime, so appointments with Dr. Pierce were difficult, but I could still start the medication while continuing on the herbs.

Emily had left for Ohio with her parents to visit family over New Year's Eve. We'd only been dating for a few months and the trip had been planned since before we met. Nevertheless, it made me realize how much I missed her. I found myself dwelling on the fact that I would eat alone that night while my girlfriend was in another state. On impulse, I went online and started pricing flights from Ohio to Chicago. Surprisingly, some good rates were out there. I got her on the phone to find out which airport was closest to her. She wasn't really close to any airport. I let her know that if she wanted to come home early, I'd pay for the ticket. But after evaluating our options we decided it best for her to stay. I would see her soon.

Around five PM on New Year's Eve, things got a little out of control for me. My bowels decided they were in charge while I was maneuvering around the apartment on my scooter. I kicked that puppy into high gear to make it into the bathroom in time. I really didn't think I'd make it, but thankfully I did. I scooted back out to the living room when I suddenly felt the urge to return to the bathroom. Too late this time. Uggh! What a mess I have to clean up. This unpleasant cycle happened a few more times and I knew something was up (or down as the case was). Knowing I should probably share this with someone, I called Emily. My sister and mother were out at New Year's Eve celebrations and I couldn't get a hold of them. I got Emily on the phone and shared with her what had happened. I knew it wasn't a particularly romantic subject matter for a New Year's Eve phone call, but I had to tell someone. On one hand she wished she could be here to help me; on the other she was glad not to have to deal with the stink and mess.

I wasn't in a position myself to clean up the trail I had left, so I just decided to try to lay down for a while. Sometime during the night, the urge hit me again. While trying to slide out of bed and onto my scooter, I missed and hit the floor. This triggered a violent reaction in my bowels and they evacuated right there on the floor and on me. I ended up lying in the filth all night long. What a nice New Year's Eve that was. When morning came, I called my sister and mother to let them know what had happened. They were upset that I had waited that long to tell them. I just figured I'd let them sleep. They both made their way over to the apartment. Kim was the closest and first on the scene. What a sight! She and Joe helped me clean up and set me up on the couch.

During this sick stage, I grew really weak. I felt like I had no strength or control of anything. I just felt so horrible. One thing that kept me going was the thought of reuniting with Emily when she returned from her trip.

COUCH POTATO

On my couch, I could at least finally rest. The first day of 2006 was looking better already. Of course, I had to be back at work the next day. I'd never taken a sick day in nearly eight years. It just wasn't in my DNA, and made me remember how my dad used to come in to work even after chemo treatments. I wasn't fighting a silent killer like he had, so I prepped myself to "man up" for my return to the office. I tried to get back on the scooter. One...Two...Three, STAND! My legs had no energy, no strength. I couldn't even get off of the couch an inch.

"Could someone stay and help me, today?" I asked my family.

Humbling. I had just gotten used to not being able to drive myself around.

My new campsite on the couch was not only my living room, but also my dining room and bathroom. I assured myself this was just temporary, though. I would rest up for the day and be ready to hit the ground running tomorrow.

Yawn. Slowly opening my sleep-crusted eyes, I reached for my cell phone to check the time. O man, it was five o'clock! Kim would be here to pick me up for work in one hour. I started to get up and get ready. One.....Two....Three, STAND! Wow, I appeared to be weaker than yesterday. Hearing a commotion, my mom rushed in from the spare bedroom.

"What's wrong?" she asked.

"I can't get up. I need to get ready for work," I croaked.

"O Randy, you need to stay home today," she replied.

"What are you doing here?" I asked.

"We knew you would need help, so I decided to stay."

I guess that was a good idea, but I really thought I would be better by the morning.

"Would you like some breakfast?" she offered.

As she prepared breakfast for me, I called Kim to let her know I wouldn't be in today. She figured that. My family took care of the details while I must've been out of it the day before.

Breakfast arrived in bed, or in couch, you might say. Yum, broccoli. All I had in the house was food for the Chinese herbal diet. I started to dig in. Are you kidding me? I couldn't hold onto the fork. I tried countless times, to no avail. My mom finally came over and gave me a hand, feeding me as she did no doubt when I was a baby. Thankfully, she didn't make any airplane noises when shoveling in each bite. Drinking was much the same. I couldn't hold onto a cup securely enough to drink. So she helped me with that, too. This was even more humbling and tougher to deal with than loss of bowel control, which at least could be blamed on medication side effects. This newest development just flat out sucked! What was I supposed to do: not eat, not drink? I had to figure out how to deal with this obstacle now. That seemed to be the recurring theme to my life. Pondering this brings me back to a time in my life that first introduced me to the overcomer mind set.

During my freshmen year of high school, I went out for the football team. I really wasn't versed on the finer points of the game, but I knew I wanted to play. Many of the other guys had years of earlier experience on the local team. Going through a summer of double session practices was the hardest thing I had had to endure in my life to that point. I just didn't know if I'd make it. Somehow I made it through that grueling summer and into my freshman years of school and regular after school practices.

Yes, it was the simpler times of my football career, but it wasn't simpler for me. I struggled with learning the plays and being able to incorporate them along with the proper blocking techniques. It's said offensive linemen are some of the smartest players, but that was not true of me. After a few games and wallowing on the "B" team, I decided to quit. My frustration boiled over one day and that's what I did. The coaches, obviously seeing some potential I did not, talked to me to see what the problem was. I told them: I couldn't remember the plays, I felt stupid not knowing what to do each play.

Hearing this, the coaches came up with a game plan. They would type up the plays and tape them to wrist bands. This way when the play was called in the huddle, all I had to do was look at my wrist to know what to do. Taking that idea and implementing it was just what I needed. By the end of the year I was on the "A" team and playing with confidence. My coaches taught me a valuable lesson that I would carry with me for the rest of my life. When difficulties arise, take a step back and assess the situation. Quitting will get you nowhere. There's always a different point of view.

Taking a step back and a deep breath allows our minds and spirits to relax and pave the way for a new point of view to settle in. The new viewpoint may come from a coach, a TV show, a friend or simply a gut feeling. Either way it's a new way to look at things. Who knows what will happen with this new perspective? It could be as simple as figuring out a new way to battle a physical challenge or it may turn out to be the latest, greatest invention.

Stepping back. Taking a breath. These simple steps made receiving help with my eating and drinking easier to swallow. I'll say this: having good people around also calmed this battle.

Going from a normal routine of working five days a week to just sitting on the couch watching mindless TV all day was nearly driving me crazy. Every night I'd go to sleep and plan on getting up in the morning to go on with my life as usual. But every morning I'd wake up to find myself in the same situation. The only reason I could get through the day was the hope that things were going to change.

By my second week of 24/7 couch time, my family thought I should go to the hospital. I didn't feel like going. I was sure I'd get better on my own. During this time, my mom noticed that an area of skin on my backside had turned black and was macerated. This definitely had her concerned. Not being able to see it myself or to feel any discomfort,

I wasn't too worried. It was tough enough to be bedridden without having to add something new I couldn't see or feel into the mix.

The next day, it was time for a shift change. Emily would stay overnight and leave for work in the morning when my mom showed up. My mom came stocked with a bag of tricks she had picked up at the local medical supplies store. She had discussed my backside with them at the store. How's that for a mother taking an interest in her son's butt? They told her it sounded like a bed sore and gave her the proper equipment, bandages and such, to care for the area. Armed with this knowledge, she applied a dressing on the area. This would need to be done every day. Also, I was to stay off the sore as much as I could. I chalk it up to another lesson learned. I was surprised to hear that I could get a bed sore. I thought that was a myth--kind of like bed bugs (which it turns out are not fictional either). And I truly thought only older people could get them. Go figure; I was wrong again.

A couple of days later, my mom purchased a nice big comfortable recliner for me to stay on instead of my nasty old couch. What a difference! It made sleeping at night a lot more comfortable. The problem I had that continued to disrupt my sleep was bladder control. If I was too sound asleep, I would wake up wet. Otherwise, I would wake up numerous times through the night to pee. Ideally, I wanted a full night of sleep without waking up to pee and to not wake up completely wet. So before falling completely asleep, I said a little prayer that God would grant me those two desires.

I groggily stirred at six o'clock the next morning, realizing I had made it all night without waking up. To my astonishment, I was also dry as a bone. How exciting! I shared the good news with Emily before she left for work and got to share the news with my mom when she came. I think they both were mostly excited because they would not have to help clean me up.

By midmorning, I still hadn't peed. Even though I felt the urge to go, I couldn't. It even kind of hurt. My mom prodded me to call Dr. Lee. I finally relented and dialed him up. He feared my kidneys might be shutting down and recommended going to the hospital. I asked him what other choices I had. In keeping with the all-natural diet, he instructed me to eat warm watermelon. That sounded like a better alternative. I hung up the phone with him and shared the information with my mom.

Despite my distaste for the hospital, I started thinking that would probably be the best idea. So, we called Kim at work. Before we could tell her, she told us that she had just spoken with Dr. Lee and he really thought I should go into the hospital. Hearing again that my kidneys might be shutting down was the deciding factor. I decided to bypass an ambulance and insisted they drive me. No real reason for this other than my obstinate pride.

While waiting for my ride, I gave Emily a call to let her know what was happening. I left a rather calm message, informing her she didn't need to come over after work because I'd probably be in the hospital still. I wasn't quite sure, but we thought my kidneys might be shutting down.

As soon as I hung up, I broke down. I'm not much of a crier, but the flood gates opened up. Not being sure of my fate shook me to my very core. Could this be my end? It was nice having my mom here to help comfort me during this dark time. After my few minutes of fear and pity, I gathered myself and reaffirmed to myself that everything would work out.

In the emergency room, a nurse entered asking the usual questions. Learning that my bladder hadn't emptied in nearly seventeen hours, she put a catheter in me. Hooray—another new experience! I really didn't care how awkward that was. Getting my bladder drained was all I had on my mind. So much urine came out she had to put on a new bag part of the way through. Finally, relief! With my immediate pain subsided, I could rest easier.

The doctor recommended a quick CAT scan to check my kidneys. Though there was nothing to worry about from the scan, the doctor thought I should stay and meet with some other doctors in the coming days. What did I have to lose? Plus, it would give those close to me a break from some of the unpleasant tasks that I continued to need done for me.

Emily showed up while I was waiting to be admitted. She let me know how much my voice message had freaked her out. She had a hard time reconciling the gravity of the message (that I was on my way to the emergency room because my kidneys might be shutting down) with my rather calm, matter-of-fact delivery style. I had thought that leaving her a calm, straight-forward message was good on my part. Boy, was I wrong. All the message did was worry her. She was at work and had no way to reach me. In her mind, she was thinking that I might have been dying. Even though that was my fear, I did not think the message would parlay that. At any rate, I did feel much better when she arrived. Life is sweeter when she's around. She helped the hours waiting for a room seem like . . . well, they still seemed like hours; it was just nice being with her.

I finally got a room and was able to get some rest,

at least as much rest as I could being holed up in a hospital. The morning brought the day shift nurses who, despite the uncomfortable situation, made me feel right at home. They informed me that it would be a busy day. I would have a number of doctors coming to visit. But, first things first, they explained how the meals work. It was just like room service. When I was ready to eat, I just had to call the kitchen and place the order from the menu. Sounded easy enough to me. I was skeptical about the quality of the food but happily conceded that it was pretty good after all. And not just 'good for a hospital.' It was just good. Period.

My first visitor of the day was a wound care nurse. She came to check out my bed sore. After rolling me to my side and receiving the full moon view, she started prodding the sore or as it was now referred to "the wound." She determined it was a Stage 4, which is the worst stage. The skin on top was black which meant it was dead. Also, it was pretty large, as far as bedsores go: about the size of a half-dollar. We formulated, and soon implemented, a plan of attack. While it sucked not having feeling below my waist, I decided that scraping off dead skin was not a process I wanted to feel.

The next doctor on the docket was an urologist, or as I like say, a pee doctor. There wasn't much physical poking or prodding with this one, but I'd say he asked more than his fair share of probing questions. He determined what meds I needed to start taking.

The worst part about being in the hospital was daytime TV. It was bad enough being stuck at home watching it, but I at least had cable and many more choices. Reading a book did not present a viable alternative amid the distractions of a busy hospital. So, pretty much, my fun for the day consisted of flipping channels until the next doctor.

The next doctor was an infectious disease doctor. I really hoped this ID doctor would be better than the others I had seen, and so in my head, I started calling him Dr. Hope. We started by summarizing up all my health problems. He then continued with the usual neurological examination and on to treatment. Since I had already tested positive for Lyme disease, Dr. Hope and his team recommended they treat me for it. There was definite surprise on my face. I knew that test hadn't been FDA-approved, so I had some misgivings. He explained his reasoning like this: FDA-approved or not, if my case were brought before a court of law, the central question would not be the validity of the Lyme test, but why I hadn't been treated when it was a known diagnosis. I informed him that I would need to think about it. My thought process included looping in Kim and letting her do some research on the medication.

Typically, Kim was nothing, if not thorough. On top of her own research, she reached out to Dr. Pierce and Dr. Lee for their input, prolonging the verdict for another day or so. No matter to me; I just wanted to make this call with my eyes wide open.

When I informed Dr. Hope that I wasn't sure about taking the medication and was doing more research on it first, he seemed a little put off. I'm sure he was thinking, "Who is this guy who feels he has to research my recommendation?" At this point in the game, I really didn't care what kind of reactions I got from doctors. I wasn't trying to be a jerk, but this was my body and I was going to do what I thought was best. I elected to do the research, and at the end of the day, my gut would know what to do.

I did eventually decide to start treatment. It required a PICC line, a tube that runs through the vein in my arm and nearly to my heart, to be inserted. It sounded a little weird, and possibly a little uncomfortable, but it sure beat getting stuck with a needle every day.

With the PICC line in place, Dr. Hope scheduled me to start the Lyme meds (via drip) the following day. My heart boiled with emotions: nervousness, excitement, fear, just to name a few. I really wanted this treatment to work, but was apprehensive that it would not. On the one hand, the prospect of getting better excited me and on the other hand, I recalled how sick I had fallen after the last time I started new meds. But as the old adage goes: nothing ventured, nothing gained. I ventured.

Hot Spot

After a few days with no negative side effects from the new meds, relief set in. And some more good news. Dr. Hope approved my release with home health care. I had a hospital bed with an air mattress delivered to my apartment. Emily and my mom would switch shifts taking care of me again. I got a first-class ride home in an ambulance. Unfortunately, since the trip wasn't an emergency, they weren't able to turn on the siren and lights — a bit disappointing. I liked the idea of an ambulance ride with all the bells and whistles. If I had to do it, might as well do it right.

Back at home, I could rest easy, so to speak. I had to be rotated from side to side every couple of hours to relieve pressure from the wound. This was especially fun for Emily, since it required her to get up every two hours to turn me. Like a trooper, she did this without complaint, though it took its toll. She set up camp in my room, while my bulky hospital bed nested in the living room. One night, she slept through one of her 'turning' alarms. I heard it; she did not. I called her name several times to try and wake her. She didn't even acknowledge my voice with a grunt or make the slightest movement. Finally, not knowing what else to do, I yelled out. "Is that Matthew McConaughey naked out here?!" To *that*, she responded. I knew that would get her attention.

During this time at home, I had a nurse coming in two to three days a week to keep an eye on the wound, draw blood once a week for tests, and provide other assistance as needed. I also had therapists coming in to work with me. Some of the simplest tasks weren't so simple anymore. I knew I had to keep working to get better. As the saying goes, "you get what you give." I wasn't about to give less than 100%. Though it would have been easy to lie there all day doing nothing and get waited on hand and foot, I was raised to always push forward. Even up into to his last days, my dad lived the greatest example of pushing through all the crap life throws at you.

A clip from the movie, *Remember the Titans*, is indicative of my attitude. Gerry Bertier had become paralyzed after a car accident. His coach was talking to him in the hospital as though this was a death sentence. He responded, "Coach, I'm hurt; not dead." That's my attitude, as long as I have breath, I'm going to live life and overcome every obstacle.

Realizing my insurance would only allow so many visits from home health, my nurse helped us figure out a game plan on what to do next. It sounded like a nursing home would be my next resting spot--yet another new adventure on this unpredictable path. By this time, I was growing accustomed to having my preconceived notions dashed. So while it occurred to me that a nursing home was an old people deal, I was also willing to entertain the idea if it would get me well again.

After days of waiting for insurance approval, I had to wait several more days for a bed to open at the home. That struck me as rather morbid. How does a bed open up at a nursing home? Death? Hopefully, that wasn't the case.

It only took two days before that bed opened up. Even though we were waiting, we had not packed. So whatever I thought I would need, I threw into two bags. I definitely wouldn't need a razor, being as I had not shaved in a few weeks. I figured why shave? It's not like I'm going to pick up women. Plus, I'm not able to do the shaving myself. The few times I had tried shaving during this ordeal, I had to enlist either Emily or my mom to help. I've gotten over the fact I need help with simple things, but it's scary having someone shave you. Plus, with winter at hand, a nice beard made sense.

Another siren-less ambulance trip later, I arrived at the nursing home. As I was wheeled down to my room, I felt like I was in the movie Cocoon--so many gray heads turning to watch the new boy. Unsure of how long I'd be there, I decided to set up camp and introduce myself to my roommate. He was probably the next youngest patient, in his fifties. We exchanged stories, and I soon realized he'd had a rough go and wasn't afraid to complain about it. To make matters worse, he liked the room hot. Keeping the room warm would have been fine, but I felt as though I was on a vacation in hell. The bright spot in this hell hole was the view. I was next to a window and had a view of a Hooters restaurant being built a football field's distance away. Now I could dream of hot wings every day of my stay.

I was curious to learn what this place had in store for me. Bad food was the first item on the menu, and you know by now how important food is to me. Next, a consultation with the head of therapy. She was a pleasant English lady, excited at the chance to work with someone younger for a change. Some physical tests were given to see what kind of work would need to be done with me. My insurance company allowed only one hour of therapy per day, perhaps because it was riskier for the average nursing home patient to exercise any longer. My therapist was great though, and gave me some extra equipment, such as a Thera-Band, hand gripper, and a lightweight dumbbell. It was humbling to be in the position of having to use two pound dumbbells for some exercises. I couldn't believe how weak I had become, though I appreciated the extra attention I was receiving. They were giving me every opportunity to succeed.

I didn't have a family doctor while at the nursing home and needed one to see me while there. So another doctor whom I had encountered at the hospital saw me. I inwardly rolled my eyes when I first realized she'd be taking care of me. Back in the hospital, she had come in on a night when I had a room full of family and friends. I was in an ornery mood, as I often am when surrounded by loved ones, so when she had asked me what was going on, I retorted with a smart-aleck comment about why I couldn't walk. She responded by saying she did not have any time for this nonsense. Anger flared up. I wanted to tell her to leave my room and never come back. But my calmer, more civilized side won out and I apologized to her and smoothed things out. As with most doctors I'd met, she felt the need to throw out a diagnosis at me: MS once again. Why do doctors feel the need to diagnose right away? I added that to my list of frustrations. I just knew in my gut MS was not the right diagnosis. I knew the right answer was out there and we would one day find it.

One day, Emily brought me some exciting yet scary news. Her parents were coming up to visit me. They would bring lunch and we'd all dine in the cafeteria. I had wanted to meet her parents but this was no way to impress them. I guess I would see what kind of people they really were, if they accepted me as I was. I was in a nursing home, wearing workout clothes, and hadn't shaved in over a month. Emily, my mom, and I picked out a lunch table and waited for her parents to arrive. I was so nervous. I spied them walking up the path with pizza in hand. My excitement over the good food definitely won out over my initial anxiety about meeting them. As I sat there eating, I felt as though I was under a bright spotlight in an interrogation room. They were not grilling me with questions. It was just the pressure I was putting on myself that made me imagine it worse than it was.

Our lunch was cut short by a therapy session. The session was on transferring out of the wheelchair onto an exercise mat. After my leg exercises were finished, we had just a few minutes for some trunk exercises before heading off to occupational therapy. In OT, we worked on arm strengthening and some hand coordination. I could tell I was getting better, but everything was still really hard.

Back in my room, I was excited to see Emily had stuck around. Not only did I get to hang out with her, I got to find out the truth on what her parents thought about me. She let me know they thought I was really nice. I guess I was afraid they would see me in a wheelchair, in a nursing home and tell their daughter to run.

I had survived the week in hell. It hadn't been easy, especially when there were no visitors. I kept pumping good music through my head phones and that seemed to help in the down times. There wasn't much else to do during the 17 hours a day you are awake.

For some reason, my IV medication was forgotten one morning. I gave them a window of a few hours, thinking maybe the staff was just busy and would get to the medication a little bit late, but I realized now I needed to push the issue and get my medication. A transporter showed up to bring me down to therapy. But his first order of business was to bring me to the head nurse and get my IV hooked up.

While the nurse was preparing to put the medication in my arm, I had a feeling something wasn't right. I watched, but I couldn't figure it out. On the way down to therapy, I kept getting choked up, like I couldn't really catch my breath and had a weird feeling in my chest. This was really odd, but I pushed through as much as I could to be able to get in my therapy session. My therapist instantly knew something was wrong and had transport quickly bring me back down to the nurse. The whole ordeal began to freak me out. The nurse unhooked me from the IV and sent for an ambulance to bring me to the ER. A few minutes after the removal of the IV, my breathing started to regulate. I was relieved that the worst was over and I wasn't dying. The EMTs arrived and carted me away. Feeling better, I was able to enjoy the ride. Finally an ambulance ride with lights and sirens like I had wanted!

The bright side to being in the hospital again would be the good food, although I would have to endure more tests, including an EKG and CAT scan. The nursing home had called my mom and told her of the situation. So she and my sister were up at the hospital most of the day. Emily was told after work and she came right over. She stayed with me well into the night. I can only imagine what she must be thinking about me and all of this craziness. I kept telling her I would get better and walk again. Then things like this kept happening-- emergency room visits, nursing home stays. I wasn't sure how, but I had to keep the faith that I was going to beat this. Whatever THIS is. Not just for myself now, but for Emily.

I was excited to see Dr. Hope again. The last time I saw him I was unable to wiggle my toes. Such a simple task, but being able to do it now was a huge accomplishment for me. I wanted to show off my progress.

The first doctor I saw was an associate of Dr. Hope.

I didn't care. I was just excited to show anyone I could now wiggle my toes and I showed him. He had remembered my condition before, so he celebrated with me. He said he couldn't wait to share the news with Dr. Hope. Finally, Dr. Hope arrived. Toes came out again, wiggling furiously. This really excited him. We talked about what had happened to bring me in again. The tests were inconclusive. Also, he didn't think it was an allergic reaction to my medication since I'd been on it for a few weeks and had no side effects. He planned to get me back on the meds and keep me in the hospital for a few days to keep an eye on me. He speculated that I had suffered an air embolism. He didn't expound on it more, but threw in that it could have killed me. That which does not kill me only makes me stronger, right? It's a nice saying, but going through anything that could kill you still sucks.

After a week in the hospital, it was back to the nursing home for me. I was not looking forward to it. Here, I had my own room, room service, and people at my beck and call. At the nursing home, I shared the room with a crotchety old guy, choked down the slime that passed for food, and waited for the bitching and moaning old fogeys to settle down and take their naps before I could get help. Don't get me wrong, I love and respect the older generation. But being in this environment also made me a little crotchety.

Everyone seemed excited to see me back. The head nurse was happy she hadn't killed me. The therapists were glad to be manipulating younger, more supple flesh again. And the nurses loved that I didn't bitch and moan.

This time around my roommate situation improved. I started off with a nice little old man named Roscoe. Every time I hear that name I think of the kooky country cop from the old TV show, "Dukes of Hazard." After a few days, he was discharged. It was bittersweet. I was happy for him to go home, but didn't want to get stuck with a bad roommate. To my surprise, I made it a couple of days with the room all to myself. Sadly, one day a lady across the hall passed away. I didn't have to see her dead body, but there were family members and a member of the clergy that were in the room for awhile. Finally, the coroner made it and wheeled her out of the room. I wasn't ready for that, I admit. I guess you have to be prepared for that to happen in such a place. The bed she had vacated was quickly filled by another lady who seemed a bit off. She would yell stuff so loud the whole wing could hear her.

Emily showed up after work per the usual. The lady across the hall was at it again, yelling for the nursing staff to come help her or she threatened to throw herself on the floor. She repeated this over and over, which really drew Emily's attention to the point I told her to stop staring. During her visit, I got a new roommate. Yet again, he seemed like a pleasant old man. I softly inquired if the temperature was good for him. Whew. He was fine with it. Perhaps this stay would prove much better. I knew it was too good to be true, though. It wasn't my roommate that was the issue this night. The lady across the hall decided to start yelling again. I didn't get much sleep that night, and at breakfast the lady started screaming again. She again threatened to throw herself out of her chair onto the floor. Knowing she had dementia, I was a little sympathetic. But I found myself saying internally, "Do it!" I know you think that's so wrong; I would normally, too. You never know how you will respond to a situation until faced with it. Her outbursts only served to remind me that, indeed, this spot was hellish and that I did not belong here. I was determined to improve quickly so I could get out of there.

OH JOY

A lady from the front office came down to my room and informed me that MarianJoy, a rehab hospital, had a bed open for me and I had to be there in the afternoon. Wow, that was quick. I wasn't sure I was ready to move again. Although I didn't like staying at the nursing home, I thought I'd be here for a while longer, be able to get stronger, work out more. At that moment, my therapist showed up to congratulate me on the next step. She told me that I was ready for this. She was so excited for me to get this opportunity. "MarianJoy is one of the best rehab hospitals in this state," she said. Hearing that helped calm some of my nervousness. It also helped to learn that I had a mutual friend with one of the EMTs who came to transfer me to the facility and the other played football at Lockport.

At MarianJoy, I landed a "room with a view" on the third floor. Granted, my window view wasn't as spicy as the Hooter's view, but it would suffice. I, at least, saw some green grass. I'm not sure if it was the excitement of this new challenge, or the fact I was awoken numerous times throughout the night by the nursing staff, or perhaps my roommate's heavy snoring, but I barely slept a wink that night. No time to contemplate that. By 6:30, my breakfast tray had arrived. As usual, I found myself judging the home by the quality of the food. My breakfast fare included pancakes and sausage links that would rival an IHOP or Denny's. Not bad. I might actually enjoy this place.

Next on my plate was meeting the doctor I'd be working with during my stay here, Dr. Martin. He met with all of his patients everyday — usually for just a couple of minutes. On my first day, he spent a little more time probing the details of my case and schooling me on how things worked around the facility. He clued me in to the battery of tests they would run throughout my stay. His first goal was to get me off of the permanent catheter I had been on. He scheduled a bladder function test. As nice as it had been not having to think about peeing, I was ready to ditch the ever-present bag of urine.

I next met my nurse, who presented me with a daily schedule. Boy, did I like that. Finally, a regimented day. Internally, I sighed in relief, "Yes, normalcy!" At this point, it was time to get ready for my 'normal' day. Getting dressed for the day meant I started out naked. A few months ago, this would have been a really uncomfortable situation, but not anymore. I'd grown to be comfortable with who I was, where I was. Even naked.

They wheeled me down to therapy, but it didn't help that there was a line of wheelchairs waiting to get on the elevator. This only prolonged my nervous excitement, and once again, I realized I was the young one among my cohorts. There were a lot of people in the therapy room. It sucked that so many people needed rehab, but I took it as a good sign that MarianJoy must know what they're doing.

A very nice woman named Kelly introduced herself and informed me that she was my therapist. Kelly just happened to have a student from a university working with her for the next six weeks, oddly enough, also named Kelly. After our introductions, she asked me to wheel over to the exercise mat for some stretches. First things first, she wanted to hear all I could share about my illness and my goals from physical therapy. All I could share for sure about my illness was that it was neurological and we were not sure exactly what it was. As for my PT goal, "To walk again," I simply declared. She didn't seem shaken by my declaration, which was reassuring. After a few stretches, we moved on to some evaluative exercises. This was immediately followed by occupational therapy. They did NOT play games around here; your day was FILLED with therapy.

The OT side wasn't nearly as big or as crowded as the PT side. My OT therapist was a girl named

Ryan and her sidekick Sandy. As in PT, Ryan and Sandy inquired about my physical state and OT goals. To be honest, I hadn't given much thought to my goals except my mantra "to walk again." I guess I had a one track mind. The OT evaluation included tests for hand strength, sensation, and coordination. Humbling is how I'd describe that session. It made me realize that I had more to work on than just walking. I was relieved that lunch time was just around the corner.

The transporter (or as I liked to call her "bell hop") broke in on my mindless TV break after lunch to pick me up for more therapy. Getting pushed around was nice, but I felt up for more independence. So I asked what I could do to go on my own. This required special approval from my therapists, which was easily granted. They already sensed I could handle wheeling around MarianJoy on my own. I was thrilled. This was almost as freeing as the day I got my driver's license. Well, not quite that nice, but freeing none the less. After my two therapy sessions, I wheeled quickly past all the people still bound to a transport and down to another elevator that I got to use myself.

With my first day of therapy on the books, I could honestly say I was worn out, yet excited to be there. Everyone was so nice, therapy had been challenging, and it all helped get me into a good mental state. To top it all off, I got to talk with

Emily on the phone that night. Hearing her voice was a perfect way to end the day.

The next day was bladder-centric. Dr. Martin really wanted to get me off of the permanent catheter. After therapy, the glamorous agenda consisted of having my catheter removed, my bladder drained and my middle poked and prodded for bladder sensation. Although I was by this time comfortable with being naked, it was a bit disconcerting to have a whole team of professionals messing with my "junk." I guess it was the price to pay to get rid of that bag. The tests revealed that my bladder was in good shape, all things considered. Since I still couldn't pee on my own, they showed me how to intermittently cath myself. It was a Friday and I had the rest of the day to myself. I would get an hour of therapy tomorrow, but most exciting of all, I would have visitors. What a great couple of days: good food, good doctor, good therapy, and no more bag of pee.

Waking up with excitement in a hospital is a foreign thought, but that's how I felt that Saturday morning. I wasn't quite sure who all was coming, but I knew at least Emily would be here. Sure enough, my beautiful girlfriend was the first to arrive. We visited for a while in my room, exchanging I love yous and I missed yous. Two more friends, Bob and Carmen, joined us in the tiny, crowded room, so we moved into one of the larger visitor suites down the hall. It was great to sit around the table and play catch up. The last month had been crazy for me. So hearing what was going on with my friends helped me to think about others and get my mind off of all that I was dealing with. Of course, questions did come my way, but I didn't mind sharing my experiences and thoughts of this new place.

The weekend passed all too quickly and it was back to the grind for me. After a full week of therapy, I not only felt stronger but also more comfortable with all of the staff. So comfortable, in fact, that one of the therapists shared some jokes with me. A personal favorite: "What kind of socks does a pirate wear? . . . . Rrrrrrgyle!" I love lame jokes! From then on, she shared every lame joke she could recall.

On Friday, Kelly let me know that we were expecting nice weather over the weekend and that if I wanted to get out and wheel around with a guest I could. You better believe I made plans. I hadn't been outside just for the sake of being outside in quite some time.

Saturday quickly filled up with visitors. I met with some family and friends in the cafeteria and talked every one into a walk outside. Emily pushed me along the walkway until we came upon a nice resting spot. Once there, we talked and caught up on the last few days. During our conversation, Emily and I realized that this was the first time since we started dating that we had been outside together. How crazy is that? Eventually the wind drove us back indoors and everyone started to disperse not long after.

Over the weekend, I gained a new roommate, Kafui, who was originally from Africa. He turned out to be a real keeper. Up until then all my roommates had been pretty hard to handle. But Kafui was a talker and very upbeat to boot. Although I had only been to Africa one time, he talked of his home land with me every day. Not only that, he had a great outlook on life and wasn't afraid to share it. How great to finally have a like-minded roommate.

The following week in therapy I was able to get in a standing machine, which locks your legs into place and lets your body get used to standing. Also, we put on some leg braces and walked some in the parallel bars. That felt so good! To go from sitting all the time to standing and walking was amazing. It was like seeing my future open up in front of me—a future I was sure would include the ability to walk, no wait, RUN again.

Another type of therapy was added to the schedule: mental. I had an appointment with a psychologist and wasn't quite sure what to expect.

Would I lie down on a couch and talk about my childhood? I didn't lie down and we didn't talk about my childhood, but it was an outlet to talk about all the stuff that I'd been through related to my disability. I know she thought something was wrong with me because I was so upbeat. There was no real "down" time to talk about. I told her every time I start to get down about my situation I quickly change my thoughts to something positive. In fact, my mom was there for one session and backed me up. The psychologist gave me some reading materials to help with handling a disability. I guess it was good to have this outlet as well.

Later in the week, Kelly informed me that I could get a day pass on a coming weekend to get out with Emily. All that we needed to do was have Emily come in to learn how to help me get in and out of the car and a few other details with handling the wheelchair. Emily was already coming in all next week since it was spring break for her, so that worked out perfectly. As soon as I got upstairs, I gave her a call to share the news. She was so excited! Finally, a whole day just she and I get to be together!

Such a big week! I got to see Emily every day. I had a field trip planned for all day Sunday, and I was fitted for my own personal leg braces to be made. Emily showed up early enough to go to my first therapy session. Not only did she get to see me in action, but I got to show her off to my therapists. I wasn't sure if I was more excited to have Emily see me stand and walk, or simply that I got to be with her all day. Either way, I felt like a kid on Christmas morning, I couldn't lose.

After introducing Emily to the Kellys, we got busy with my hour-long session. Emily got to see me stand and walk for the first time, which I thought was pretty awesome. That was a milestone in our relationship.

The next morning, I met with a fill-in doctor while Dr. Martin was on vacation. He wanted to talk to me about my wound. He saw that I'd had it for a couple of months and thought surgery would be best. I asked what that would entail and discovered it meant being laid up on my stomach for about a month. That was the gist of it. After he left the room, I was pissed! I'd been here for over two weeks and insurance would only allow 30 days maximum for life. So basically, I wasted my whole time here. My nurse came into my room not long after the doctor left. He could tell I was visibly upset, so we talked about things for a bit. He sympathized with me, but agreed with the doctor that maybe surgery would be best. Not willing to accept that I told him, "You just watch! My wound will get better." What a start to the day! I now had some angry energy to burn off at therapy, so I guess that was the silver lining.

That evening, I had a wound update with a nurse. The update consisted of taking measurements, snapping a photo of it, and redressing it. She first took the measurements: width, length, and depth. Before even checking them against last week's numbers, I knew it had gotten smaller. The two of us were really excited, especially after the doctor's surgical recommendation. When she was snapping the picture, I smiled real big for the camera. I knew the picture was of my backside, but I still liked to smile when they took the picture. I slept well knowing things were getting better.

On Friday, Emily and I learned how to get me in and out of the car safely as well as how to maneuver curbs and such. That wasn't too hard. All my other therapy sessions the rest of the day were kind of a blur in anticipation of my big date Sunday.

Emily arrived nice and early and got me signed out. The closer we got to the outside, the more excited I got. We managed to get me slid into the car and buckled in relatively smoothly. This consisted of Emily gently inserting one end of a slide board beneath my butt cheek and extending the board toward the car seat. I then had to grab on to her and the car door frame for support as I slid into position on the car seat: After some wiggling and folding of my legs to fit in the front seat, Emily removed the board and stowed it and my wheelchair in the truck. This was our first time driving somewhere together — another great milestone for us.

We met Emily's mom for breakfast. It was my first time being out in public in a wheel chair. Nearly everyone at MarianJoy was in a wheelchair. There you didn't think about it, but out in the real world, I was the odd man out.

After breakfast, we headed to my apartment. It felt so good to be back. Also kind of surreal, especially considering that I still had one more week at MarianJoy and then some time at a skilled facility, a.k.a. nursing home. Not until I was done at the nursing home would it be time to start my real life again. So in a way, I felt like a visitor in my own home. Without a real plan for our date, we just kind of hung out around the house. Unsure why, I suddenly decided to buzz my beard off. Everyone at MarianJoy had wanted me to shave, joking about wanting to see what I looked like underneath that woolly mess of hair. With it buzzed off, I finally felt the air on my face, which was weird. After a while my sister and her fiancé popped by for a visit. They were surprised to see my face again, so to speak. The day passed far too quickly, and soon it was time to pack it up. On our way back, we stopped for some Mexican food, my favorite. We drove through at a local joint and ate in the parking lot. I learned fajitas are not a good car food. Plus, my stomach didn't take too kindly to it either. I had a bit of a blow out while getting out of the car at MarianJoy. What a pleasant end to a great day! Once upstairs I had a nurse's aide help clean me up. With that mess behind me, I was ready for my last week.

That week would be spent preparing me to return home. At the end of the week, my braces would be completed and we'd need to make sure they worked properly. With just a few days left Dr. Martin informed me that they would remove my PICC line later that day. He said I had had the medication long enough. Although I was ready to be without this line hanging out of my arm, I was worried. I feverishly called Dr. Hope since I wasn't sure if he was ready to stop the treatments. I got through to a nurse with whom I shared the news. She told me to call back when I was done with therapy and she would have an answer for me.

The answer came loud and clear: do NOT pull the PICC line. Since Dr. Hope had seen continual progress, he was not ready to stop treatment. This made me feel really good. I had a doctor that was on my side. Crisis averted!

I still had a couple of days of therapy, so I was ready to take full advantage of this time. In OT, they wanted me to try cooking. I got to make a couple of omelets. They smelled so good that I was asked to whip up a couple more for a patient and therapist. It felt good to be cooking again.

After breakfast, Dr. Martin had a talk with me. He and his team, after spending some time evaluating my case, felt confident that I had MS. I disagreed and told him so, but what did that matter? I would be out in a matter of days and would never see him again, so I really did not care what he thought of my disagreeing with him. He'd been a great doctor to deal with this whole time, and this one disagreement would not change my opinion of him or this place. But, I'm not going to lie, it pissed me off: yet another doctor with what I thought was a bum diagnosis.

By my last day, sadness had crept in. I had come to really like my therapists, doctor, nurses, and fellow patients. This place had become a home to me. I guess that will happen when you live somewhere for a whole month and they see you at your most vulnerable. I made my bittersweet farewells, sorry to say yet more goodbyes, but anticipating what would be in store on the next leg of this journey.

BEAR

A nursing facility link to MarianJoy was my next destination. I met with the person in charge for the weekend before getting whisked away to my palatial suite. I joke, but the rooms were big compared with MarianJoy. I could tell early on I was going to have to be my own advocate here. The mattress they had was not an air mattress, which I definitely needed since I still had the wound. However, it was the weekend staff in charge and they hadn't been informed of my special needs. My mom followed the ambulance from MarianJoy with my bags of stuff, so she made her way in and started putting my things away. Since I arrived on a Saturday, there wouldn't be anything for me to do until Monday. I'd just be hanging out in my room with whoever came to visit. While I was resting, a nurse came in to take my vitals and inform me of a few things. Her main point was that since I had a PICC line I'd have to get an x-ray to make sure the line was where they wanted it to be. If not, they'd pull it and put in a new one. Are you kidding me? I felt like this was just stupid-a waste of time and money. I argued my point with the nurse as best I could. I got pretty hot about it, but lost out in the end. That was their policy and no way around it, especially with the weekend staff.

While lying in bed waiting for the x-ray company to come, I talked with my roommate to find out more about the place. He'd been here for a couple of weeks and really didn't have a problem with it. "We'll see," I thought. So far, they had not gotten off on the right foot with me. The only good thing with the x-ray was that I was able to stay in bed while it was administered. That didn't take long, but I was still worked up from having to do it in the first place. No decision would be made about the line until Monday when the doctor was back in. To make my first day here even worse, they didn't have the catheters I needed to go to the bathroom. Having a full bladder and no way to empty it made me even more grumpy. I was so frustrated and did not want to be there. Even with my mom around part of the time, there wasn't much she could do for me. She just tried to calm me down. It helped a little bit, but I still wanted out. She waited for Emily to show up before she left.

I gave Emily a run-down of the situation and how badly I just wanted to go home. She encouraged and comforted me. She reminded me why I was there—to get better. My goal was to walk again and I shouldn't let these things get in my way. Even though her talk helped me gain perspective, I still had stuff to deal with. Emily stayed as late as she could since she had a previous engagement the next day. After I knew she'd arrived safely home, I went to sleep wondering if joy really does come in the morning.

Sunday morning arrived after a restless night of sleep. I wouldn't say I woke up joyful, but I definitely was not enraged like I was the day before. Peace came for the moment. Eating alone in the room was prohibited, so I took my first meal under the watchful eye of a nurse. The food critic in me knew I wasn't at MarianJoy anymore. I'd liken breakfast to a school lunch. Remember the days we got French toast sticks and sausage links? It was just like that. Kim and Joe made their way out to see me. They ended up being the only visitors since Emily had an orchestra performance. At least I had a therapy session to look forward to the next day.

I started the day with OT. It was a big room with a bunch of therapeutic equipment. As before, my therapist wanted to know my goals. At MarianJoy, my only goal was to walk again. That had to change. Yes, walking was my main goal, but with living at home again within sight, I knew I needed to get better with some simple tasks. At MarianJoy, they worked with me on things such as transferring in and out of bed, transferring onto a shower bench, getting on to and off of a commode.

I guess those are the three necessities: sleep, shower, and poop. So on top of working on my strength and dexterity, I let her know that I wanted to work on those things for when I went home. The hour buzzed by and PT was next. Yeah, this is where I really wanted to be. I brought my leg braces down to show that I was ready to get on my feet again. After our initial pleasantries, I let her know my goal in PT was to walk again. She said she was on board with that.

We started with getting me on the mat and stretching me out. We had just enough time to do some trunk exercises and then it was over. That was it, two hours of therapy and now I was done for the day. What a far cry from my month at MarianJoy. I was back upstairs with the rest of the day ahead of me and nothing to do. I thanked God for headphones and good music I could listen to while blocking out the world around me for a while.

Nudged awake, I was startled to say the least. I had obviously fallen asleep while just relaxing. My pointy-fingered friend was none other than the doctor whom I'd be working with during my stay. He shared with me what he knew about my case, "You have MS..."

Before he got any further, I spoke up and corrected him. "I have MS-like symptoms, but we're still working to find exactly what I have."

"We know for sure I have Lyme disease," I told him. I got the sense he didn't appreciate being corrected, especially by the patient. He moved on from there and discussed my bladder. I told him that I cath myself a few times a day but pointed out that I had not done so since I'd been here. They didn't have the correct catheters. He said he would look into that for me. He also wanted to switch me to a different bladder medication. That was pretty much it with him. I prayed he'd get right on my catheter cause. I really wanted to pee!

This doctor turned out to be a big disappointment. First, it took a couple more days to get the right catheters. And it wasn't the doctor that got the ball rolling. It was one of the nurses that had become very friendly and sympathetic toward me. So thanks to her, I finally got to empty my bladder.

Within a day of switching bladder meds, I peed all over myself. This went on for a few more days before I demanded to get back on the previous medication. At the end of the week, I told the doctor I really wanted to leave. Not only did I feel my health was being compromised, but I just really missed home, so the doctor said he would get the ball rolling on Monday.

During my crazy first week, I got my third

roommate. He had been in a horrific car accident and was in pretty bad shape. His name was Barry. Barry had to wear a stiff plastic support brace whenever he went to therapy and it looked very painful to maneuver in and out of. He just powered through, though, which impressed me.

Barry told me his friends called him Bear. I'd stick with calling him Barry. He was easy enough to talk to and we quickly moved beyond the small talk and on to deeper topics. He seemed balanced and down to earth but it was apparent that the accident had shaken him to his core and he readily shared his feelings about it. His openness helped me to put my situation in perspective.

We both kept it light, too, and shared similar tastes in humor. My beard was long gone by this time, but Barry still had a full one. I told him I was glad it covered up his ugly mug. Barry dished the grief right back. Once when I was primping in the bathroom getting ready for a visit with Emily, Barry called out, "You can try as hard as you like, you won't cover up the ugly." We were comfortable ripping on one another like that, as brothers would do.

When Barry first moved in you could tell he was loved by many. His wife taped all the cards sent to him on the wall. It looked like she had wallpapered his side of the room. After a while, I saw why. He was a great person to know. Also, I admired his determination.

During my time there, my friend Garrett came by often. His job was right around the corner. He would stop by after work and hang out before heading home. He and his wife came by one evening when Emily was there and brought some good local Chicago area pizzas. While enjoying this treat, Garrett offered some to Barry. He gladly took a few pieces as he had been on a feeding tube since the accident. I think Garrett just ordered himself up a new friend. I think he was angling to become his friend just so he could call him Bear.

Two more Barry connections occurred after we had both been released from the nursing home.

> The last stop on my whirlwind tour of hospitals and nursing homes last year brought a great roommate my way. It was not the norm to have a young man of 27 in a nursing home, but a man of 46 to be there at the same time were 1 in a million. Although I was only there for 2 weeks we fast became friendly. Now when I left I had all his contact info. And soon after unpacking, his info had been lost. I recently received a message from him on this blog and can't wait to hear more from him. So Barry hopefully you're checking this blog. You can send email to randy@randybeal.com. We still need to do dinner at Al's.

I just got a phone call from my sister. She had some exciting news for me. She had just finished an interview with a guy that would be starting for us next week. Who is the man? None other than Barry's father-in-law. When I was told this I was so excited. I have so badly wanted to get back in touch with him, now there's no reason I can't. It's great that this worked out!

Though I was only in that nursing home for two weeks, Barry and I became close. I never quite picked up the habit of calling him Bear, but to this day, I consider him a true friend.

A STEP FORWARD

My first night back home, it seemed strange that I would be staying there overnight. "For real, I don't have to be back before curfew?" I thought to myself. At bed time, Emily assisted me in getting ready for my first night back in my own bed.

How nice it was to wake up when my body was rested and ready to get up. I did not realize how much noise there actually was in all the places I had slept over the past three months, whether it was the nurses in the hallway or the raucous snoring of my roommates or the lady across the hall yelling. Later that day, a home health nurse stopped by to draw blood, administer my medication, and change the dressing on my wound. Now that Emily was living with me, she got the unenviable job of changing the wound dressing every day. The nurse walked her through the steps for doing that. She watched and learned what to do. Emily rocks! Once a week, a nurse would come over to draw blood and do a wound assessment. Since I got the wound by way of pressure on my butt, I had to get out of the wheelchair and lie down during the day and sleep on my stomach at night. I'd figure a routine out soon enough. Once the nurse left, I got my Emily time. I loved getting to hang out with her. She would be back at work soon and I would be hearing from therapy about setting up a schedule.

Our first morning of getting up early was upon us and it felt extra early that day. Emily helped me get dressed and stretched before getting me into the chair. After the rest of the morning to-dos were out of the way, it was time for Emily to go to work and for me to see how a day by myself would be. I knew one big thing for me would be getting into bed to give my butt a rest, so around nine, I got back into bed for a few hours. That worked out well, being as Oprah aired at that time. While I was lying down, a call from the rehab facility came in. They wanted to set up a time for me to come in. They would pick me up every day I had therapy, which was nice. After getting that all set up, I got myself out of bed. Transferring back into the wheelchair wasn't so hard. As usual, I had built up obstacles in my mind to make the prospect of being alone unsettling. But I had to admit that being home by myself wasn't too bad.

I arrived at the OT appointment without a glitch, despite my usual hang ups. My occupational therapist let me know she'd be with me in a few minutes. This gave me time to relax and check out what they had the other patients doing. It was a different environment here. I was the only one in a wheelchair. We spent the first part of my session talking about where I was physically, how I had gotten to this point, and my goals going forward. Of course I was very vocal about my main goal of walking. In a typical therapist fashion, she didn't seem fazed by that goal and said, "Let's get to work on that." She tested my upper body strength, my sensation level, and my trunk stability. The hour flew by.

"I'll see you on Friday," I said after she wheeled me to the PT room. My therapist got right to it. We discussed my goals. Sounding like a broken record, I told her I want to walk. Plain and simple. We spent the rest of the hour doing some trunk exercises. She told me to come Friday ready to work.

It was great to be home, but a little boring as well, so I really enjoyed seeing everyone at therapy. That Friday, at OT, we worked on some trunk exercises and finished the session with some hand coordination exercises. Those included activities you might see a young child doing like putting marbles and blocks in the right holes. I had to teach my hands to do the basics all over again-- kind of humbling for me still.

At PT, we started off by stretching me and decided to stick with some leg exercises. We would work on standing next week and I would need to bring my leg braces then. I couldn't wait to get on my feet a few days a week. She had told me to come ready to work, and she meant it. Thankfully, I had all weekend to rest up. Like clockwork, the drivers came to get me after the session. Being picked up and dropped off for therapy was great. I felt some independence with that. I left the apartment myself and returned to the apartment myself. Although small, those little things helped me through the day. I was excited to share my progress with Emily when she returned home-- another day closer to my dream of walking again. I was starting to feel almost back to normal. I had a full week home and a sense of routine returning.

I was in therapy for five months and we focused on improving my standing skills with occasional walking sessions. Eventually, we worked up to walking once a week. When I say walking, it was only a few steps at a time. Eleven steps were the most I did during this time. I was happy to be making progress, but it still seemed it wasn't going far or fast enough. And of course, all this time I was also racking up charges for the therapy. Insurance had covered the first few weeks, but I was on my own for the rest. I came to the conclusion that I needed to give up therapy, more for financial reasons than anything. I spent a few weeks at home, but soon got restless. My sister, Kim, suggested I come in to work at our family business and she would help me do some therapy on our own there.

Kim picked me up—in her tiny sports car, mind you. Transferring in and out of that thing was no walk in the park. It was weird being back in the shop and being in a wheelchair and talking with guys I hadn't seen for months. I told them I'd be up and walking in no time. Everyone was very supportive. Since I was trying to do therapy on my own away from trained therapists, I started things out slowly and began with some basic exercises.

At one of my regular appointments with Dr. Hope, he recommended I see a neurologist, and there was one in the same building that he trusted. As I trusted Dr. Hope, I willingly went to see this neurologist. By this time, I had the whole doctor dance down to a science. Handing over the chronological health history that Kim had typed up simplified the process. The new doctor read it and told us we're better off going to a hospital downtown. So once again, I scheduled time with another neurologist.

They say the third time's the charm, but I was hoping the fifth neurologist would be the charm for me, hence another doctor nick name. After meeting with me and reviewing my case, Dr. Charm ordered up an MRI. You'll recall I don't have the best track record with MRIs, so this time we wised up and got some sedation before going in. I don't remember the MRI at all, which is how it should be. I do remember the results though.

TWO STEPS BACK

It was September 20, 2006, a Thursday evening. I was lying in bed when Dr. Charm called. She had reviewed the MRI, saw the lesions on my brain, and could only conclude what I'd heard before and what I dreaded hearing again: it was MS. I told her OK, but I disagreed. She was wrong; she had to be. She went on to recommend further tests after hearing my disagreement. This news was numbing, filling me with unrest and sending me into a mental tail-spin. Early on in the sickness, I had submersed myself in worship music, trusting that God would cure me. I was starting to feel better physically and see some progress in healing, but this new diagnosis led me to question myself. Had I neglected God? Had I become complacent with my condition? I started to feel like maybe I had turned my back on God and hearing the MS diagnosis again was Him slapping me in the face and saying, "What about me?"

After the initial shock of yet another set-back, I got to thinking about it as less of a punishment and more of an opportunity. Dr. Hope once told me, "Randy, you've got the greatest physician of all on your side." He wasn't talking about himself, though I knew he was in my corner. He meant the Great Physician, of course, and was referring to my faith in God. I reflected back to something I'd known all along: God put me here, in these particular circumstances, for a reason. It was to make a difference, in any way I could. I had had visions of speaking to people, even large groups, and encouraging those who have gone through similar trials. I had shelved those dreams and honestly felt like God had put those dreams away for good.

Back in my power-lifting days, I remember how some of the guys would have a coach or teammate slap them full force in the face to get fired up before a big lift. I felt this is what God was doing to me with the phone call from Dr. Charm. I had a seemingly insurmountable weight to lift: my goal of walking again. I had claimed that 2006 was my year to walk. The news that I had MS was a huge slap in the face, but one that fired me up rather than stopping me in my tracks.

The morning after the call I had a brief moment of doubt. I recorded 26 seconds worth of doubt. The gist of it was: sometimes I think I would be better off not here, as in had never been born or already dead and on the other side of this. But I never give too much space or time for such thinking, and was more than ever determined to walk again and to prove the doctors wrong.

Settling into a normal routine helped get my mind off the diagnosis. When Kim would take me to work, I set up in my dad's old office. I had a laptop and would surf news and sports for awhile, then wheel into the shop and talk to the guys. No actual work was involved. But I did strive to work my muscles. Sometimes I would do this by wheeling around, sometimes by doing hand exercises with one of those squeeze things. The plan was basically to get me out of the house and around people, but when Kim had some spare time, we would start to work on standing.

It started with putting the braces on, no easy feat when seated in the wheelchair. The braces were very Forrest Gump-like and that's what I referred to them as—my Forrest Gump braces. Once I had the braces on, which took a good 20 minutes, we practiced standing up. Most of the time, we left it at just standing up, sometimes with braces and sometimes without. I had to have the braces on, though, if I wanted to attempt steps. I could get up to 8 steps before I had to rest.

By October, we decided to kick it up a notch and take some steps without the braces. I blogged about it.

> How do you handle fear? Do you use it as motivation or do you let it cripple your life? We have the choice on how to handle it. Yesterday I had the choice to succumb to or overcome a

fear. I wanted to stand and walk without braces, but had not done so in over a year. I was afraid to crumple to the ground when trying to stand and if I did make it to a standing position what if I fell trying to walk? Well, I decided to go for it; the reward would blow the risk out of the water. And boy was I right. This particular situation brought me to think about all the times I faced a fear and overcame it. Not once did I look back with regret, but with fulfillment and excitement. And all the times I succumbed, I wish I had them to do all over again. Lord, help me to always live life with excitement and face my fears with fervor.

Work became known as Kim's Boot Camp to me. She worked me hard. I'm normally pretty hard on myself, but Kim was always there to kick my butt and push me to do more. She wanted me to walk as badly as I wanted to and never let me give up. Here's how it went down: Kim would walk ahead of the walker and serve as the carrot to my horse, constantly urging me forward and demanding more of me. I would start in the wheel chair, stand up using my walker, and start taking as many steps as I could. My mom followed behind with the chair, ready to spot me if I fell or just needed to rest awhile. The work-outs continued at home. Emily helped steady my walker and I'd stand, even take some steps.

One night, I was watching TV with Emily in our

living room. Out of nowhere, I got this overwhelming feeling of being tired of being in the wheelchair. Up until this point, I knew the chair was a necessity for me to get around and I was fine with that. Maybe it was because we'd been standing (no braces, just the walker) for several days now. It was a freeing feeling. In fact, I'd say I got addicted to it and we started a more rigorous routine the next day. We got up at 4am everyday and I was standing by 4:30am. It was such a good feeling to be up on my feet. Every chance we got, I wanted to stand. Now I was sure Kim's Boot Camp would be focusing more on walking. Every time I got up, I would ask God "Is today the day?" I always imagined myself walking, kind of like Forrest Gump: starting out slow and then into an all out sprint. "Run, Randy, Run!" Emily cheers in the background. In fact, while lying in bed at home, I had these near out of body experiences. I would get up out of bed and walk into the kitchen of our apartment, where Emily's fixing dinner. She would cry out, "You're walking! You're walking!" To me, it was just what was supposed to be, no big deal. I just got up and walked.

Naturally, all this was very encouraging and I felt good about the progress I was making. Walking was coming soon to a theater near me, only this time it wouldn't be Forrest Gump, but Randy Beal taking those strides and running the length of that football field.

Soon after, I had an appointment with my neurologist in Chicago. I hadn't seen her since August. She had me do some physical tests to see what had gotten better, worse or stayed the same. Everything she checked, from leg strength to coordination to my vision, all got better. This was really confusing for her. She didn't know how I could get better. That moment was really good for me mentally. I really felt validated that perhaps MS wasn't so final a diagnosis after all. I'd had some depressing days over the last couple of months and I felt as if I broke through that slump finally. I had been speaking life into my situation again and truly was convinced my walking days were right around the corner. On top of all of this, I received my handicap parking placard in the mail. It was a temporary one which was good for 6 months. That was the way my doctor filled it out, not as a permanent. This was cool, that Dr. Hope believed in me and felt I was going to walk again. It also happened to be close to the holiday season--a time for miracles. I really thought it was time for my Christmas miracle, even up to the last day of 2006!

AGAIN AND AGAIN

When 2007 rolled over without my miracle, I was bummed, but not discouraged. I determined to just keep working that much harder. I wasn't walking, but there was some good news. Emily excitedly reported that my wound was completely closed up, about a full year from the date of its discovery. We were cautiously optimistic that the worst of my, er, behind was, well, *behind* us. This was a great victory and helped soften the blow of not getting my miracle in 2006.

By early February of 2007, I took a whopping 51 steps in one day. I was high as a kite. The next week I reached my all time high number of steps: 202. I felt like nothing could stop me. But then, the following week on my 151st step, I tweaked my back and fell backwards into the chair. I wasn't in excruciating pain, but enough to know that I had damaged something. I tried to stand again, but had to abandon it. This was bad. I thought a couple minutes of rest might help, but it was no use. All my months of hard work and all those steps seemed to come to a crashing halt.

It took me a week after the tweak to get to the point

where I could stand again. Kim talked me into going to the chiropractor. I found one near our office. Not only did they do chiropractic, but they also did therapy. They put me on a 12 week plan for getting my back straightened out.

One doctor, Dr. Justen, was particularly excited to be working with me. When we first met we went over my current health situation. He then asked, "Your goal is to get rid of the back pain?"

"Yep, that's what I want."

He replied, "That's not our goal. Of course, we want to help your back pain, but you walking out of here is our goal."

Inside, I shouted a resounding, "YES!"

He followed up with, "It's gonna be hard work when you're here; deal with it." So we went through the initial routine-electric stimulation to the back, an aqua bed, and an adjustment. Next onto a bike, one I could pedal from my chair. I needed a good amount of assistance pedaling, but they also made me work through most of it. They worked me hard.

On one particularly bad day, I was feeling beat from the get go and told Kim I wasn't going in. I had to cancel therapy that day as well. Staying home alone all day feeling like crap brought me to another break down moment. I was confused and depressed, not knowing what God wanted from me. I thought I was close to figuring things out, but really I didn't know who I was anymore. What was my life about? I needed guidance, help, direction. Honestly, I felt like my life sucked. I sat around doing nothing. I tried to push myself most days, but this one really brought me down. At that moment, I didn't see my way out of that dark place, but thankfully my disposition won't allow me to stay there too long. I sometimes lose sight of the carrot, but I know it's there in front of me and if I keep moving it will come into view again.

As I got to know Dr. Justen more, I shared more of my medical history with him. I noticed a change in his attitude after reading the files. His mindset changed from "you'll walk again" to "we're gonna work you hard and see what happens."

And it was hard work. I got some chiropractic work first and then onto therapy for an hour. I knew walking again wouldn't happen in just three days a week there, so I worked out while in my chair and even lying down in bed. Despite the doctor's seeming loss of vigor about my walking again, I was determined to beat this even more. I had faith in the miraculous work God could do. With those two things: determination and faith, I'd made it through the darkest hours in 2006, and they would see me through to the end. I was determined to work harder today than I did yesterday.

I've been working hard, first learning to live life with a disability and now to overcome and defeat my challenge. Last year when things looked really bleak I kept confessing my faith in God and my belief in a miracle healing for my life. It was easy back then to confess those things. Now that I've learned to live with this I feel like I've gone as far as confessing and believing alone can get me. That doesn't mean to stop those, but I know there's more involved now. The battle I've been fighting more than ever, is the one about trust. I keep hearing a little whisper, saying "trust Me." I know the next step in my recovery, physical and spiritual, is to trust God. Easier said than done. To trust there has to be an action. Ever do the 'trust fall' where you turn your back on a group of people and have to fall into their arms? That was always a scary exercise, but it always worked out. You would think it easier to trust the God that created you, but that always seems toughest. So I'm hoping to overcome my biggest challenge, 'Trust God!' I really need to do it before that whisper gets any louder. I guess it's like any relationship, it's great to hear 'I love you', but the next step is to show you love that person. God I love you.........

Back in January when I was bedridden, I was able

to believe God for a miracle. I had made a lot of progress since then. I was still in the wheelchair, but was in a lot better situation. I had learned to live with my condition and work around the rough patches. And I found that I didn't go to God as much, or call on Him, or seek His guidance. But I know I needed Him at all times in my life: good, bad, in between.

I had just finished my third week of therapy and saw some progress. My legs and core were getting stronger. Each time I had gone I noticed at least a slight improvement. Any was better than none! One exercise I did at therapy was bike pedaling. My therapist always helped by holding my feet on the pedals, and he helped me get full revolutions. I bought a pedaller for me to do at home. One morning before going in to the office, I wanted to try it and see what I could do myself, so I wheeled up to it and got my feet settled on the pedals and away I went. I pedaled five revolutions and could have done more, but stopped to not wear my legs out before therapy.

At an appointment with Dr. Charm, she did the usual neurological tests (strength, vision, coordination) and went over my previous test results. Things still seemed to be inconclusive. She conferred with Dr. Hope, but to date they had no definitive answer. The plan from here was another brain MRI and some more blood work. There might even be the need for a spinal tap. She would also contact a Lyme disease specialist. This was still a tough case to crack. As long as I kept getting better, I could continue to deal with this incomplete diagnosis. My neurologist thought if nothing more definitive showed up in the tests, we would be left with calling it MS.

I went to the chiropractor twice a week now. Two to three days out of the week, I had a rough time physically: my vision was blurry and my hands and legs were extremely numb and stiff. One day, I felt so bad I thought about cancelling therapy, but decided to push through. After my therapy session, my legs were totally worn out, but I actually felt better than when I first showed up. My eyes weren't as blurry and my legs weren't as stiff. I realized it wasn't about how I felt; it just mattered that I showed up. That's a good life lesson. Just showing up is sometimes the hardest battle, but if you don't show up you'll never know what could happen. You get what you give.

At my 8 week evaluation my sister came with me to therapy and she contributed this:

Approximately 8 weeks ago I took Randy to see a chiropractor in town. He started physical therapy immediately with his attempts at the exercises being futile. Considerable assistance from the therapists was needed, he became winded almost immediately, had spasms in his legs, struggled with his "thinking" on getting his brain to tell his legs what needed to be done and had some Chris Farley like mental melt-downs when his body would not cooperate. Bringing him back to work, he had to go to bed for a couple hours just to regain some energy for the drive home. (I think after that initial session the doctors may have lowered their expectations for his improvement as well!) After a few appointments I started dropping him off and waited for the call to pick him up when therapy was finished.

Today was his 8 week re-evaluation/progress report. I decided to hang out and watch; ask the doctors some questions; and scream in Randy's ear if the need arose. Well, the need did not arise and most of the time I sat speechless watching as he worked at his exercises with little to no assistance from his trainer! Even his little "head-case melt-down" he recovered from quicker than I've ever seen! As I watched I saw the strength and control he has achieved in his legs and core; there were no spasms in his legs; and he did not become exhausted or extremely fatigued as was in the beginning.

Sometimes being the person with the condition and struggling everyday to do the most minor of things, one may not notice the improvements or not realize the magnitude. Well, today I exclaimed to Randy to be proud and excited of his improvements—it's like night and day!

Soon after, I met with my neurologist to go over my latest brain MRI results. The MRI really had no significant changes. Dr. Charm talked about what she thought of my situation. There really was no answer for sure, so after seeing the symptoms and the brain MRIs, the only thing she could think was that I had MS. There was enough uncertainty that I decided to get a couple more MRIs to look into some back issues. I truly couldn't say why at the time, but let it be said I was no longer frustrated and had not been for some time. I was very sure I didn't have MS. I knew my body better than anyone. Plus, I had a great sister who researched tirelessly for me on my health. I was going to push and push until we really found out what I was dealing with. At the end of the day I was getting better without anything other than determination and faith.

There wasn't much I could control about my condition, but I could control my reaction to it. Part of my response was never giving up, trying to find a way to make things better. That led me back to Chinese Herbal Medicine (CHM). There was no conventional medicine to help me get better but CHM offered some hope. I know I had lesions on my brain from the MRI. Basically, these were spots on my brain that were causing a breakdown to the signal my brain sends out to tell the rest of the body how it should work. This was a main reason why my body was in the shape it was in. Dr. Lee felt that CHM could eradicate lesions. He likened them to concrete: if they've been there for a while, it would take some time to remove them. You'd have to keep chipping away at them. Also, the herbs I would be taking would keep new lesions from forming. I felt comfortable going this route since I did this back in 2005 and saw good results.

I'd lived in the same 2 bedroom apartment for the past 4 years and the second bedroom had just been nothing more than a junk room. Emily and I decided we were ready for a change from the funky colors I had experimented with years earlier. We had the apartment painted a nice clean white and got rid of all junk and clutter. I say junk and clutter, but it was just stuff we didn't use or wear anymore, so we were able to bless the local thrift shop with lots of great clothes and other items. That, in itself, lifted my spirit a little. I had been in a funk for some time. All I knew to do was keep pushing and something was bound to give.

Sitting in the newly cleaned room, listening to a new download from one of my favorite Christian artists, I finally felt free. I felt like a weight had been lifted off my life. You never know how or when things will change, but keep pushing and eventually they will. I had truly felt like giving up and didn't feel I could fight anymore. But I remembered a word I kept getting through men and women of God and in my own quiet time with

God over the last 10 years. It was this: that I've got big shoulders and a lot will be put on them, but never more than I could handle. Believe me, there are days I wish I didn't have big shoulders, but when I come out of those difficult periods, I feel I'm a stronger and better person for it. So I celebrate another small victory.

I realized that the last time I walked was in February. I had taken 151 steps, but right at the end I tweaked my back pretty bad. After nearly 5 months, I knew it was time. I knew it was going to be tough and I had to start my goals low. I can be so hard on myself and have a tendency to beat myself up if I don't meet or exceed goals, so I set my goal at 3 consecutive steps. I walked 4 and a total of 9 for the day. I was thrilled with that. It felt so good to be walking again. Back at home I set a goal of 5; I walked 8 and after that did another 8, almost doubling the previous day's grand total of 9. Although it was a far cry from my all time record of 202, I felt well on my way to that.

The day arrived for the dreaded spinal tap. As they prepped me on the bed, we were laughing, just making jokes and having a good time. Stressful situations are easier for me to swallow with a hearty dash of laughter. While we were talking, I asked if my sister could take video or at least pictures of the experience. She agreed to pictures. Two of them stand out to me. One is of the needle and the other is of the needle in my back while fluid was being drained into a tube. (I know my sister and I are a little off kilter. I would have it no other way.) This time, the tap was a breeze--no pain involved at all. This made me wonder what that previous doctor was doing. I was expecting the results the following week.

The results weren't what I had hoped for. As with every test, I was waiting for something out of the ordinary to be diagnosed. This time it was the same old story: MS. I decided to roll with that as a diagnosis, even though I was skeptical. Either way I was going to beat this. I was going to start an MS med to stop or at least slow down the progression of the disease. The Chinese herbs were helping me to lose weight and get a little stronger. Along with the MS med, Dr. Charm started me on an anti-depressant. Being on an MS med increases the likelihood of depression, so she was being proactive in prescribing me the anti-depressant.

Getting back on my feet walking had been tough--I'll even say discouraging at times. But in typical Beal fashion, I kept my head up and kept pushing and speaking faith.

In early September, even though I wasn't feeling the greatest, I kept on pushing, and was able to get my highest quantity of steps in nearly 6 months: 40. Wow, what a feeling! I was able to get 12 steps in a row too, when my recent high was 9. Even the quality of the steps was better. Having a day like that helped keep me stay motivated and made those discouraging days seem like a distant memory.

I'd be done with my chiropractor sessions after 12 weeks, and I wasn't up and walking like the chiro first thought. That was a bit ambitious of him to say, but that attitude is what I needed around me at the time. Though it had been good for me physically and mentally there, I still needed more therapy if I were going to walk again. I decided that I would start going back to the rehab facility I first went to after my whirlwind tour to get more intensive therapy.

SHAKY & BROKEN

Being back at rehab felt good. I saw some familiar faces—some of my former drivers and my prior therapists. I was given new therapists this time around. In a way, it was a new lease, a second chance, and I was motivated to push toward my goal of walking. Even more, Emily really hammered home a critical point to me at the time that has stuck with me. She said I needed to get my head out of the "one day" and enjoy today. So I tried to incorporate that view into this next phase of the journey.

It didn't take long for the newness to wear off. Nearly 10 days later my blog entry read:

> For the past month or so I've been home every day. That means not going to work. That's a big reason for that dry period I was in. It's been tough to figure out a routine. I do still go to therapy twice a week and the other days are on me to work out at home, which I do. But when I'm done the appeal is there to just watch TV and relax. I mean c'mon Oprah's on at nine. :-) I admit it I'm an Oprah junkie. So, I'm starting to get into a routine of sitting in my home office and reading or writing or something

constructive every day. Today I did a puzzle challenge online to help my brain stay sharp or get sharp, depending on who you ask. The days of sitting in front of the TV weren't helping my waistline either. Although we have only healthy foods in the apartment, eating too much of anything will fatten you up. I had lost a good amount of weight this year, but I've added some back on recently so we're being careful in that area too. I believe that dry season was God sent. For one, I'm so hard on myself all the time that I needed a break. Plus, I've been able to figure what's most important and get things in order. Sometimes we are so bent on staying busy that just because we're busy doesn't mean we're productive. I plan on being productive during this new season.

This unmotivated state wasn't something I was used to and somewhere I wouldn't stay forever. I just wasn't sure how or when I'd shake that funk. A few e-mails and comments with encouragements were good enough for me to slowly start doing something about it. I thought to myself, "I'm not setting the world on fire, but I'm slowly getting my feet back on solid ground. "

I was back to using my leg braces, between the parallel bars. I took a few steps forward and a few steps back, literally. I had never done that in therapy before, but I did really well with it. I felt I was getting stronger all around physically, able to stand a little longer and better each time.

> Today in occupational therapy my heart was broken. While I sat working out my arms I felt these little eyes peering at me. I looked over and saw a little girl no more than three years old struggling to walk with a walker. This immediately touched me. I've had the joys of running and playing sports and never having to think about the next step I was to take. It looked like this girl never had those chances, and I don't know if she ever will. My prayer at that moment was that if God could give her those abilities, I would gladly take her infirmities and be trapped in this chair forever. Even now I'm broken up thinking of that little girl. I know God doesn't require that kind of sacrifice in order to do that kind of miracle. I do think it does take that kind of prayer, that kind of passion to tap the heart of God. God, allow me that passion in every area of life especially my prayers.

Going through what I have has definitely opened my heart and made me more compassionate toward others.

My therapist suggested I give aqua therapy a try. Getting into the pool for therapy was a whole new experience for me. Knowing I had MS-like symptoms and people with MS and hot settings did not mix well, this concerned me. Heat usually exacerbated my symptoms. In intense heat, my

140

vision would become really blurry and my body would become extremely weak.

When I first wheeled into the room with the pool, the warmth got to me and I felt horrible. I knew I had to push through and truly give this a shot. My therapist and pool hand helped me transfer from my chair into the pool via a mechanical lifting arm with a chair that would go underwater.   I was slowly lowered into the water, which was 90+ degrees. It felt weird on my skin, but quickly my body adjusted.   My therapist got me set up for some standing along the side of the pool. It took me a minute to get situated to stand and then we got a few stands in. It definitely was easier to get into a standing position, but once up my legs wanted to quickly buckle. We then moved on to some other leg exercises. With a pool noodle wrapped around my back, I did some flutter, scissor, and bicycle kicks. The good thing with doing these in the pool was when my legs became tired I was able to still do the movements.

After the session, I discussed my feelings about the pool. I felt better physically afterwards than I did going in. Plus, it boosted my confidence. In a way it was a "see, I told you so" moment for me to all the doctors. The fact that I did so well in hot water seemed to be an indication that this wasn't MS. To this day, no one can explain why I did so well in hot water.

Neurologically, I had been regressing more over the past few months. My head had become shaky and my right arm, too. It used to be just my left arm that was shaky. Then it moved to my right arm and eyes. Then to both arms, eyes, and my head. That was definitely difficult to handle. This stressed me out. Feeling stronger but actually regressing in some areas felt like a wash.

Learning not to sweat the small stuff is a tough process. I've always been a worrier, someone that stressed over the smallest of things. I wavered between learning to relax and succumbing to my old nature and stressing over small things. Emily quoted me on our way to a wonderful birthday dinner for my sister's father-in-law. She remembered my telling her when we first started dating and she would share her frustrations from work. I told her that she was allowing herself to be stressed and really at the end of the day what does it matter? She could choose how she responded to those situations. She should choose to relax and not sweat it. I needed to take my own advice and choose to relax and not sweat the small stuff. It's my choice on how I respond to these situations.

Will I walk again? This is a question I've been asked many times. But what gets me most is when I ask myself that very question. My standard answer to others is "for sure, it's just a long process, but I will walk again." I've wrestled with this thought often, during the good and bad times. It's not like I'm slipping today and having a bad day. It's just that I can't shake this question. I'm never going to give up, slow down, or accept this as my fate. I know deep down in my gut there's an answer to this. I'm not sure when, where, or how it will come, but it's out there. I know I've come this far with good ol' determination and an all loving God. Maybe I haven't allowed Him into this process enough (or at all sometimes), but I know that's the only way to get my answer.

As I pondered these things, my sister sent me a scripture that helped:

> *"Wait patiently for the LORD. Be brave and courageous. Yes, wait patiently for the LORD."*
> *Psalms 27:14*

Sometimes, our fears creep in because it seems like God is taking too long to answer us. Is He out there? Hold on. He will answer you, so you must trust Him while you wait. I broke out of my questioning mode *knowing* that I would walk again.

Wheel Marks

Therapy was going great and I especially loved pool days. Things were looking good, but I noticed what I thought was a bad side-effect from the MS medication. It turned me into a bobble-head. In fact, I did a video demo on my blog to show my readers how it was particularly noticeable when I tried to take a drink of water. So the MS med was my scapegoat and I stopped taking it. Unfortunately, the shakes didn't stop. The medication had nothing to do with it. I would have to eventually admit that my condition was worsening, causing the general shakiness too.

Dr. Hope was determined to get an answer for me. He had talked about me going to Mayo Clinic a couple months back. I always thought I'd end up going there, but it was my last resort. It was almost an admission that I was giving up and I think I was secretly fearful that I would hear what I didn't want to hear.

It didn't take long for him to get an appointment. I had planned to travel down to my friend's wedding in Indianapolis in mid-June. Emily and I went down to Indy on the 12th. I was in the wedding party and the rehearsal dinner was on the 13th. The wedding was on June 14th. Dr. Hope got me the appointment for June 18th. I literally had one day of rest before we had to be on the road again. In hindsight, the timing worked great. Had there been too much time before the appointment, I'm sure I would have stressed and brooded. The wedding festivities helped take my mind off myself and celebrate others.

In the meantime, my sister was pregnant and scheduled to be induced on June 17th as well. I'll always look at that day as a gift in more ways than one. Six years to the date we had lost our father. It was a dark day indeed. But Bianca's birth turned d-day to B-day and has been cause for celebration ever since. While I wished I could be home for the birth, I knew that I had to pursue the answer we would find at Mayo. Another gift awaited me there.

When we got back from Indianapolis, our parking garage security guard, Murle, saw us and came over to ask how things were going. I told him we were going up to Mayo Clinic. He wished us well and hoped we got our answer there.

Murle and other guards and attendants have known me since I moved into the apartment building 5 years earlier. They've seen me when I could walk on my own and drive wherever I wanted. They saw my steps slow down and become wobbly. They knew when my truck got outfitted with hand controls so I could still drive. And they watched while my motor skills declined until I was wheelchair bound. All this time, they always asked me how I was doing and how they could help. They not only keep an eye out for me, they seem to genuinely care about my well-being.

Murle and his friends from the PG so impressed me with their kindness that I tried my hand at a poem on my blog. I called it "Ode to the Parking Garage"

> O the parking garage
> Where everyone knows my name
> Not just a place for the car
> But a place for conversation
>
> When I was sick
> They sent a card
> Prayers and good thoughts went up
> Not to the top floor, but to God above
>
> In the attendants and guards I found
> Not just watchmen, but friends
> When I was down
> They put a smile on my face
>
> Staying in the chair is not an option
> Pushing me to not just walk, but run is their goal
> When my brain seemed unused
> Ideas and thoughts they used to stretch my mind

O how I wish everyone had a parking garage
But wait. They do.
It may not be where you park your car
But where you get coffee, lunch, or go to church

Make yourself friendly
And there you'll find a friend
Open your mouth and speak
And they will speak back

Before heading up to Mayo, I felt God speaking to me. As in the "Footprints" poem, He said He was going to set me back down. The poem is familiar but I repeat it here for you to read again. Imagine you have been unable to walk for several years as you read it.

One night I dreamed a dream.
I was walking along the beach with my Lord. Across the dark sky flashed scenes from my life. For each scene, I noticed two sets of footprints in the sand, one belonging to me and one to my Lord.

When the last scene of my life shot before me I looked back at the footprints in the sand. There was only one set of footprints. I realized that this was at the lowest and saddest times of my life. This always bothered me and I questioned the Lord about my dilemma.

"Lord, You told me when I decided to follow You, You would walk and talk with me all the way. But I'm aware that during the most troublesome times of my life there is only one set of footprints. I just don't understand why, when I need You most, You leave me."

He whispered, "My precious child, I love you and will never leave you, never, ever, during your trials and testings. When you saw only one set of footprints, It was then that I carried you."

This encouraged me greatly. I was going to get things figured out and cured in Minnesota. I was going to make footprints again.

What a beautiful day to travel! After 7 hours in our spacious rental car, we made it into our hotel room for a few minutes of unwind time, for me at least. Emily unpacked and went to get us some dinner. What a great woman! She is my Superwoman. I appreciated her during this key time more than ever.

My nerves were long gone. I was content and confident, feeling like I was at the right place at the right time. The morning of my appointment was a sunny, beautiful day. Even if it had been a dark, dreary day it would have been sunny to me. I was ready to move forward.

We handed over my 5″ binder of health info (test

results, MRI images, travel history, etc.) prepared by my sister to the front desk for the doctor to review. My anticipation was great, but this appointment felt like so many others I'd had over the years. It always started with the nurse checking my vitals and asking some other general questions.

We spent around two hours with the neurologist. He was very thorough in his evaluation, both of me physically and of my thick binder. This was the legendary Mayo Clinic — the best of the best. I was confident they would put me on the right path to recovery. It was now time for his diagnosis.

I took a deep breath. This was a big moment--the culmination of my journey to this point. My mind raced back to the earliest days of symptoms I had brushed aside. I remembered the strange bout of Bell's Palsy and the sleeping sickness in Africa. The numbness I felt creep into my feet and legs, the blur and vision, the inexorable decline that came slowly at first and eventually robbed me of the ability to walk. I replayed every conversation I ever had about my health in my head with random taxi drivers, with Kim pouring over medical books, with family and friends, with doctors ranging from incompetent to caring and everything in between. The medical history binder was sitting on the exam table glaring at me, but I felt its weight in that moment as sure as if it was opened in my lap. All the research, every theory, however far-fetched, that might explain what I had, all the poking and prodding, Chinese herbs, therapy sessions and notes inside about to be resolved and made worth the hassle. I thought about my sister, my mom, my father who had never seen me in decline but who was certainly watching from above, Emily, all the friends that had supported me along the way, every nurse, orderly, transport worker, ambulance driver and parking attendant who had offered assistance or uttered kind words. I envisioned reporting back to them that I finally had my answer, that my stubbornness and determination would be justified. Here it was. I exhaled and had my answer.

His determination was that I had multiple sclerosis.

You might expect that I stubbornly denied or argued that diagnosis, especially given all the times I had refused to accept it before. You might expect those words to hit me like a ton of bricks and bring on a depression. You might expect confusion, hurt, anger. The last thing in the world I expected on hearing this was peace. But, there it was, staring me in the face. I felt peace. The kind that passes understanding, as the Scriptures say.

When he was telling me it was MS, a light bulb went on for me. I was suddenly in a place of total acceptance. Hearing this diagnosis from the best of the best made the words really resonate with me. I wasn't angry or distraught. At that moment, I felt like I was given the keys to live again, to not let my disability keep me down, but to really enjoy all life has to offer.

In that spirit, Emily and I decided to take a few days of vacation and relax in Minnesota. I had truly gone up expecting to be there awhile and to return with the start of a cure. Now that the pressure was off, I could just enjoy the moment.

On our way home, I was able to put into perspective what I heard from God regarding the Footprints poem. God *did* set me back down. Only it wouldn't be footprints I make in the sand, but wheel marks. God was setting me back down to live again.

Reflection

With the undiagnosed part of my life now behind me, let me take a moment to look back before moving on to the next part of my journey.

> Today is supposedly an unlucky day, Friday the 13th. I find myself to be very lucky though. Some may wonder how I can feel lucky after the hand I've been dealt. Well, although I've gone through so much, I've also learned and grown so much that I might not have if I didn't go through all of this. I'm lucky to have great friends, to have cheated death, to have realized what makes me happy, to have found love. Today I feel like the luckiest man on the face of the earth. To all my friends and family, I want to say thanks for helping me feel this way!!! May you all feel the same in your lives. God bless!

I'm thankful for every doctor I've had along the way--ones that I stuck with or not. You all played a part in my growth as a person. I know I've still got a lot of growing to do. To all my therapists, thanks for believing in me and pushing me. Although things aren't always easy, I'm thankful to have gone through what I have and come out stronger. The right attitude when facing adversity goes a long way. I'd rather be growing from the wheelchair than be walking and stagnant as a person.

Just because I choose to look at life from this perspective, doesn't mean I'm totally happy with not being able to walk. I still have those nagging 'what if' questions.

What if I started an MS medication years ago?

What if I didn't travel out of the country?

What if I went to Mayo earlier?

I wonder if any of the above would have made a difference. I guess we all ask those questions in life. If I were given the chance to have some do over moments, I'm not sure I'd do anything differently. I'm glad I kept pushing on the diagnosis, testing that it really was MS.

Life throws both good and bad your way. How you deal with each, how you change yourself instead of trying to change your circumstances, makes all the difference.

As you know by now, I like to look back on my life and assess where I am. I love where I am now. I have an amazing partner by my side in Emily, good family, and a few close friends. I do like to reflect and look back but I'm not one to dwell there. I am thankful for the challenges I have had in the past. Going through them has only made me stronger. But today, I feel I am turning the page and going to the next chapter. I don't know what the chapter is about, but I'm excited to read on. Let's see what's on the next page.

PART TWO:
DIAGNOSED

Now What?

When we returned from Mayo, it was summer break and Emily was off work. I, too, was in a summer state of mind. I let myself just relax. I definitely needed time to chill out and let the diagnosis soak in, instead of pushing through. I always felt I had to be doing something to be productive. I saw the value of being still.

I was heeding Emily's words and living in the today. We went out for dinner from time to time, or watched TV together, or just enjoyed an afternoon nap. We didn't stress about the diagnosis or even talk all that much about what was next. Having the diagnosis did not change where I was physically, so there was no need for us to dwell on it.

Emily and I went to one of her friend's weddings nearby. After getting dressed up and out to the car, I felt horrible. I was having a hard time with the wheelchair and transferring into the car, so in typical child-like fashion, I threw a fit. I didn't want to go anymore; I stressed about being a limp noodle and an adult bobble head. Finally I mustered enough strength, and with Emily's help, I got into the car. Once she got herself into the car, I complained some more. She took it all in stride, but on the road she had some words to share. "It is what it is," she said to me. "What if you are a limp noodle, bobble head? No one cares."

It didn't actually bother her or those around me. It came down to me fearing what others thought of me. After talking about it, I decided to go in to the wedding and let whatever would happen happen. During dinner my shaky hand took over and I spilled soup on my shirt a few times, but I did not let it phase me. When the entrée arrived my hands and head were still shaky, but I just pushed through and ate. Everyone at the table was not pointing and laughing at me as I feared they would. They didn't seem to care. In fact, quite the opposite, we were all laughing and having a good time.

Upon leaving, I felt like I had taken another step in living my life. Emily and I are both stubborn people, but I'll give her this one. She was right. It felt good not to care about how people would react.

Before the diagnosis, I had poured my attention into figuring out what was wrong and fixing it. Now I was starting to realize that this was more of a permanent condition. I couldn't hide behind the hope of a cure; I had to face the reality of my worsening condition.

I understood why others who faced similar despair in life would want to give up because I wanted to give up many times. I felt crappy in body and in spirit. I know I had the answer I was looking for, though it was the answer I didn't want. But now that I knew it, I could move on to the now what.

Although it gets tough to keep going sometimes, knowing there's a brighter future ahead helps. I don't know for sure what's in the future, but I choose to believe this. When I get to the point where I want to give up or end it all, I now say to myself, "Give me 10 minutes." That's usually the amount of time it takes for me to talk myself off the ledge. Positive-self talk goes a long way. You may have a different threshold, but find what it is and hang on till you get there.

My time to chill out was a great idea. But, all good things must come to an end. The problem was I had a hard time getting out of my relaxation mode. After a while, it became less about letting the news sink in and more about just being lazy. I just couldn't get motivated to do anything. I figured that when Emily went back to work at the end of summer it would be just what I needed. But, I was wrong. I was trying to get into a routine to no avail. I tried reading a book to get me jumpstarted, but only got a couple of chapters in before putting it down. I thought maybe working with a basic photo editing program would get my brain going again, but it wasn't enough. I scheduled a couple of White Sox games with my good friend Garrett, thinking maybe getting out of the house would help. I really wasn't sure what to do with my life. I knew I needed to reboot myself now.

I was not the person I used to be. When alone in my head with my internal thoughts, I didn't feel any different, but in the harsh reality of interacting with other people, I knew I was. I couldn't see well, my hearing was not that great, and my speech was slow. I hadn't found my comfort level with being around others yet. I thought I had until it was time for me to go to a Bible study and I started to freak out. Thinking about having to talk in front of people and not being able to hear everything, I got myself worked up to the point of not feeling well. I ended up not going.

When I talked with Emily about it, I broke down. She is so good to me. We talked through everything. She said I won't feel accepted by anyone else until I accept myself. So that became my new goal: to be fully comfortable with myself. Emily made me realize it's all on me. Had I gone somewhere and people pointed and laughed? No. Had anyone made fun of me because of how I talk now? No. Had I fallen out of my wheelchair in front of people? (Except for that one time she dumped me out on the street!) No. Get over yourself! I know I've battled this for some time, but I feel like I've had little bit of a break through. Needing to accept myself is very important. I understand this. It is logical and makes sense. But as hard as I am on myself I knew this would be a difficult road.

One night, Emily attended a sorority meeting of women educators. She met a woman whose husband also had MS and he went to a support group. She then asked if I would want to go to a support group. I quickly responded with a resounding, "No!"

As is usually the case, I thought about what I said after the fact. Why was I so quick to say no? Talking with other people battling the same things I am might be a good thing. I asked her what she knew and if she would find out more. I told Emily why I had responded so sharply. Going to a group would be accepting I have MS. I really thought I had already accepted this, but I guess I had not. I realized I was going to have to work harder at it than just making a mental note. I acknowledged to myself "I have MS" and tried to believe it. I guess it's like working through the stages of grief to acceptance. I made this a number one priority: to become comfortable in my own skin and to truly accept that I had MS.

ENJOY THE JOURNEY

In the spirit of living life and living it to the fullest, Emily and I decided it was time for an excursion to Chicago, despite the challenges that being disabled—*that having MS*—presented. We rolled down to the train station. The train had a wheelchair lift and a special place where I could "lock and load" for the hour plus trip. Once downtown, we met up with Bob and called for a handi-friendly taxi. It was a nice deal. I rolled up the ramp and got locked down for the ride to Millennium Park. Gotta love The Bean! We dined at a restaurant across the street, a recommendation of Bob's. Elk and rabbit sausage were featured. We were trying new things all around. After dinner, we rolled down the street to enjoy the weather and sights.

We must have gotten carried away because we realized we'd have to hustle to make the 9 pm train. We were finally able to hail a taxi after what seemed like an endless wait. Once unloaded from the taxi, Bob ran ahead to try to sweet talk the conductor into waiting for us and Carl Lewis, er,

I mean Emily, was pushing me so fast I thought we could fly home. We arrived just in time to see the train leaving the station. His dejected look told us we had missed it and would have to wait for the 11 pm train. That was fine because Bob waited with us and we got to talk and laugh some more, especially about the sprint to the train. I couldn't wait to go downtown again. It was a good experience in helping me to become comfortable with myself around groups of people.

Strangely enough, my 10 year high school reunion also helped me with expanding my comfort level. I was excited, but nervous about going. For classmates to see me in a wheelchair would be odd and uncomfortable. To be around people that only knew me when I was totally healthy would be an additional jolt.

Here's my quick synopsis of the reunion encapsulated in a blog.

> It turned out to be a late night, but well worth it. Seeing old faces was cool. I recognized some right away and others I was not so sure about. Even still it was a good time. I was afraid my wheelchair might be an uncomfortable thing. Not in the least though; no one made me feel uncomfortable about it. It was fantastic to talk to old football teammates (one of whom we

found out worked at Emily's school). Many other good friends: Vicky was now a dentist; Martino a cop. Kristy, Janine, Amy, Sandi, Pam and everyone else that made last night a success: *You guys rock!* I debated not going, but was so glad I went.

I went in with many misgivings, somewhat dreading the evening, but left so comfortable with where I was in life. My former classmates made me feel normal, like my disability was not even an issue. It wasn't an issue for them, so why should it be for me? I still wasn't sure what the future held for me, but I was starting to see that MS wasn't going to hold me back from enjoying all that life had to offer.

Before Mayo, I had been confidently telling people (including my classmates at the reunion) that I wasn't sure what I had, but I was going to beat it and would be walking again. In my mind, admitting that I had MS was admitting to defeat. It meant I'd be on MS medications and implied all the limitations I was trying so hard to fight. After Mayo, I came to a place of acceptance. Sure, I had *acknowledged* that I might possibly have MS, but I hadn't *accepted* it as a part of my DNA. I had to let it be a part of the definition of who I was — not the final word, but a defining factor. I had to face that my condition came with conditions. This was not an easy place for me to get to mentally, but once there, I discovered the diagnosis was not a death sentence. Simply put, I was just accepting my "right now" and allowing myself to live in it.

With my high school reunion behind me, I knew that another milestone wasn't too far away: my 30th birthday. When I was 18, I never thought I'd make it to 30. That seemed to be so far away. As I approached 30, I became excited. The first three decades had been an adventurous ride. I had no clue what this new decade would bring, but sign me up for the journey. Turning 30 put things into perspective for me. It taught me to relax and take each moment as it comes, to not stress so much about tomorrow.

When I used to lift weights, I would slowly build up to the heavier weight. I would work out each day and little by little demand more of myself. I'd put my reps in. Much of life can be repetitive — doing what you know is right over and over again. This builds strength for the bigger challenges. But you can't continue non-stop. Your body and your spirit require rest. You don't want to burn out. In power-lifting, we would take a break after a big meet. So it is in life. Sometimes you have to work out challenges little by little, but this prepares you for when the big challenges arrive. You power through and you overcome. The adrenaline rush of the accomplishment might tempt you to jump right on to the next big thing. Try giving yourself a break. I have always found this to refresh my spirit and build up my reserves. When ready to lift again, you need to start at a lower weight and build up to a new record. By alternating periods of intense struggle with periods of rest, you build endurance and strength.

At age 25, I stressed about life so much. I felt I should have accomplished much more. In the overall scheme of life, though, 25, or even 30, is nothing. Realizing that was like a light switch being flipped on for me. I suddenly felt a sense of perspective in my life. There were many good years ahead with much to learn and experience. Why should I stress about the little things? Heck, why should I stress about anything at all: walking, finishing this book, or having something to "show" for my years? Life isn't about the destination; it's about the journey. I, for one, am determined to enjoy the ride.

BITTERSWEET

As I'm getting older, I must be getting wiser too. I wasn't about to let the best thing in my life get away and I knew it was time to ask Emily to marry me. Here's how it went down:

I had gone with Joe to what I told Emily was a doctor's appointment. Instead, we went ring shopping. I'm pretty sure she suspected something was fishy since she and Kim always took me to appointments, not Joe. Then, a week or so later, Emily and I went to dinner at a little Italian joint across the street from our apartment building. This was a bit different from our routine of staying home Friday night. But still, by the end of the dinner I hadn't said anything. In fact, she admitted to me as we made our way home that she thought that tonight would be the night I'd propose.

When she opened the door of our apartment, she realized it WAS the night. On a table, Kim and Joe had arranged candles and roses and the ring box, prominently displayed with the lid open to show off "the rock." Emily was certainly surprised and the best part of all—she said yes!

We figured out a date for the wedding soon after: October 10, 2009. It was nice to have a date in place, which kicked off all of the planning. Emily settled on the girls she wanted as bridesmaids. With that number confirmed, I asked my guys. I asked my good friend and travel buddy, Bob, to be my best man and good friends Garrett, Adrian, and Matt to fill out the bridal party. Adrian himself was getting married in October of 2008 and a group of us were going to meet up at his wedding. It felt like my life, approaching 30, was finally going places.

Garrett, his wife Noel, Emily and I had planned to drive down to Adrian's wedding in Nashville and meet up with Matt, who was flying in from Los Angeles where he was recording a solo album. Noel, however, gave birth to their third child just days before we were to leave, so it ended up just being me and Emily driving down for the wedding.

I was looking forward to seeing Matt again. Matt and I became friends pretty quickly, and it was one of those friendships where it's so natural that you can't pinpoint when it happened. But when it happened didn't matter, I was just glad it did. Matt was a free spirit and deep thinker.

Early on in our friendship, we attended a Bible study together. I remember Matt speaking out and questioning the group about something that was read. The group became defensive, but I sat back and quietly soaked in the heated discussion that followed, impressed that Matt didn't just take things at face value or believe what someone else told him to believe. He had to kick it around a few times, and take it for a test drive.

Not too long after that, he took a literal drive to California out of the blue because that's the way he was. Although I hated having a new friend just take off, I loved that nothing would keep him down. He was yin and I was yang. Over the years, our friendship continued to grow. I loved running a sound board, and he and his cousins had a band, so there was a natural match. I went to a lot of their shows, helped set up their instruments, and on occasion ran the sound board.

Adrian's wedding was at a cool venue: an old house that had been converted into a wine bar. The wedding was outdoors on the grounds and the reception inside. Once we settled in to our spot, I gave Matt a call to see where he was. I left a message—that was certainly nothing new when trying to get a hold of Matt. I figured he was up to his usual free-spirited ways and would give me a call later. The plan was for him to ride back to IL with us the next day, but he never showed or called back. Ah, that's Matt. We chalked it up to Matt being Matt—no doubt something shiny distracted him and we'd connect with him at a later time when he'd be full of hilarious stories of his misadventures.

A few days after returning home, my sister took me to a Dr. Hope appointment. Sigh. Back to the reality of doctors and disease. In the hallway waiting to see the doctor, I noticed a couple of missed calls. Before I even had a chance to check my VM, another call came through that I answered. It was Matt's cousin. What he shared with me threw me into shock: Matt was found dead in his apartment in LA. What a devastating phone call.

Soon after getting this news, I was called into the doctor's office, still in shock and not in my usual jovial mood. As Dr. Hope is like family; he listened to me express my devastation and offered comforting words. My head was swimming with emotions.

I spent the next few days in a haze of sorrow, reflecting on our friendship and hoped that writing some thoughts down in my blog would help ease the pain. I was grateful for the memories we shared. I remembered working together at his shows. I just loved being able to play my part in seeing a friend's dream come to life. While that was fulfilling, I must say I enjoyed our time sitting around with a cup of coffee and sharing in deep conversation even more. It was rare to sit with Matt and not have the conversation get a little deep. Matt was an avid reader and recommended several books that invoked both your mental and spiritual brains. He was passionate about truth and loved to discuss life and God and what it all meant.

I went to Matt's memorial service with a heavy heart and a pit in my stomach. Matt's mom just fell into my lap and cried. She said how she wished he would have gone to the wedding and been able to drive back with us. After comforting her the best I could, it was on to his brothers. This really sucked! No words could comfort; just some hearty hugs had to suffice. I moved on to speak with some mutual friends and his cousins, who had been members of the band back in the day. Over the years, I spent some good times with them and we reminisced about those days. The service featured a video montage that brought tears and smiles. His mom's pastor brought a brief word, and a time of sharing stories followed. There were a couple of real tear-jerkers in the mix, but mostly it was stories that brought laughter.

To end the night, his former band mates reunited to play one of their songs. It was great hearing the song and thinking back to when Matt was still with us. Matt's producer brought a track of Matt singing, recorded days before his passing, and his cousins sang live along with Matt's recorded voice. It was a powerful moment. Even thinking back now, I get a little choked up. All in all, the night was a great tribute to Matt. I think about him all the time and miss him like crazy. Just being around everyone and remembering the good times did help ease the pain. Matt will always be remembered by the way we live our lives, especially when we do so to the fullest. I'm so glad I could call him friend.

Matt was always an inspiration. I loved how passionate about life he was. If he wanted to travel, he did so. I remember receiving a call from an "unknown" number randomly one weekend. It was from Matt, who was in Thailand and just wanted to say "hi." He truly was living life.

One of the last times we got together before he moved to LA, we shared our dreams. His was his music and he let me listen to some recent stuff he'd recorded and wanted my opinion. I loved the depth of his writing and musical creativity. My dream was getting this book completed. He read some of what was written and really liked it. He said, "This story needs to be told." That meant a lot to me.

Remembering Matt and writing about his life hammers home this truth: not only do we need people to accept us and be there for us, but we need to be willing to do the same. Having someone who believes in you and who champions your cause and forwards your dreams along is truly an added bonus in life. If you don't have someone like that, then maybe you need to step out and be that kind of friend for someone else first.

BUST A MOVE

My wedding to Emily was getting closer. As we already had our bridal party set, we decided not to change a thing. I was so glad I got to ask Matt to be in my wedding before he passed away. His spot in the bridal party would remain.

As a way to honor Matt and save him a place in our wedding, I ordered some small, nickel-sized charms engraved with MM on them. These were to be attached to the boutonnieres of the guys in the wedding party. This was a small token, but it meant a lot to me to still be able to have Matt play a role in my wedding.

Leaving a spot open for him was one of the easier choices. After seeing a few facilities, we chose the venue, which meant that the ceremony and reception could be held at one location. That felt good. A power wheelchair-accessible limo of some sort would be the next challenge. After doing a lot of research, we found a trolley service with a wheelchair lift that would transfer the bridal party and guests between the venue and the hotel.

Everything else was normal wedding planning stuff (cake, flowers, DJ, photographer, etc.).

Before the ceremony, I got to hang out with my groomsmen in our dressing room while Emily and her girls were doing their thing. Adrian produced a copy of Matt's last album that he had been working on when he died. Matt's cousins had finished the album and made it available to his friends and family. Listening to Matt sing while preparing for the next big step in my life felt right. It felt like Matt had finally shown up.

Some grooms get cold feet on their wedding day. I'm not sure what brings that on. Maybe thinking about how uncertain the future is. I think about *that* every day, but on this day, I thought about what I was certain of. There is one thing I am sure about and that is how much I love Emily. She has amazed me from day one. Not knowing what the future holds and voicing my concerns, she just replies, "It is what it is." She makes me feel better about things when she speaks her calming words, so just knowing she would be by my side made me confident that our future would be bright. She made me feel sure in unsure times. I couldn't wait to declare my love and devotion to her in front of our family and friends.

I had officiated Kim and Joe's wedding ceremony

nearly two years earlier, so she returned the favor and performed ours. Emily's connections in her orchestra led to a string quartet to play for the ceremony. After being pronounced husband and wife we tried to exit the ceremony side by side, but I ended up rolling over her dress on the way down the aisle. A holy hush fell on the audience, as they were unsure how to react to the awkward dance that was being played out. I backed up my chair, Emily proceeded ahead of me, and cheers erupted from our guests. My heart echoed those cheers. I had just married such an amazing woman!

Now it was time to celebrate our marriage with a reception. We had decided not to do a first dance as a couple since it would be awkward in a wheelchair. Wasn't our unrehearsed "dance" down the aisle enough? But I couldn't help but burst into a smile as I watched Emily bust a move on the dance floor. In fact, I even rolled myself out there later in the evening and was mobbed by a couple of ladies. I was truly thankful the chair had a seatbelt and I was firmly strapped in. I, for sure, would have been dragged to the floor otherwise.

One extra that Emily and I decided to add to the reception was a photo booth, complete with silly props and costumes. What a blast to watch our family and friends hamming it up for the cameras. If you weren't much of a dancer, you could definitely pose for pictures and get an instant souvenir. Plus, Emily and I got to keep copies of all the photos from the booth, too. We had so much fun just being goofballs together!

I was so grateful to have family present for my wedding. On my dad's side in particular, two of his brothers and two of my cousins came. I really missed my dad not being there, but we took a picture of the five of us Beal men that night for my wedding album. That is one of my favorite pictures. I like to imagine my dad is in the picture, too, perhaps just outside the border but looking happy for me. I'm glad I got to share the day with family.

Marrying Emily meant she was officially family to me. I also inherited her awesome parents and sister. They are very down to earth and easy to talk to. There is no judgment in their attitudes. What a great package deal I got with Emily!

Perspective

Now that I was married it made me think more about the future. Was MS going to kill me? At one low point, the thought of dying really scared me. Now, I had not only myself to worry about, but Emily, too. I wanted to live. I didn't want this disease to be the thing that separated me from the one who meant the world to me, so I keep striving to do what I can to ensure that this condition will not get the best of me.

Being married is great, but it's definitely not all roses for us. A partnership between two head-strong, stubborn people makes things interesting for sure. We joke about how we bicker like an old married couple (a la Frank and Marie Barone on "Everybody Loves Raymond"). One area where we complement each other most is our outlook on life. I'm the eternal optimist/dreamer and she is a pessimist/realist. If she keeps her expectations low, she will not be disappointed. I like to let myself hope for the best and dream about what can be. Yes, I'm let down more often than not, but I'm happy for that time I had to dream. Thinking about the impossible becoming the possible. I won't stop dreaming, but now I have a partner to comfort me when things don't work as hoped.

One dream I had expressed in a blog from 2006 seems appropriate. This was in the earlier days of our relationship and I was writing about what a great girlfriend Emily was:

> "I long for the day I can walk with her hand in hand and she doesn't need to push me."

Buying a power chair for our wedding allowed that dream to become a reality. Perhaps it wasn't in the way I'd imagined, but it felt great to be able to hold her hand as we walked down the aisle, for a second at least. Since then, we have also purchased a wheelchair-accessible van. We can now walk side by side and explore our world together. Seeing that dream come to fruition brings to mind other dreams I've had along the way.

Back in 2006, I got a tattoo, my first one. My friend, Garrett, helped me roll into the shop. I had picked a scripture.

> *"But they that wait upon the Lord shall renew their strength. They shall mount up with wings as eagles. They shall run and not be weary. They shall walk and not faint." Isaiah 40:31.*

At the time I was taking this verse rather literally and expecting I would walk any day through some miracle. Now I look back and realize that I *have* flown on eagle's wings and I *have* run. And I *am* walking each day and not fainting. It may not be in the fashion I thought it would be or on the timetable I wanted. I always had a "Lord, help me be patient . . . quickly!" mentality. But, I've come to understand that God doesn't always answer prayers with the exact wording you would expect and the interpretation of your dreams may take a wonderfully unexpected turn. True, I'm not physically walking, but being able to tell my story (and thereby help someone else write theirs) is better to me than walking through life like a zombie, not realizing or appreciating the treasures I have.

Dreaming has always kept me willing to fight another day. My dream of walking again eventually led me to become comfortable enough to accept my diagnosis and to find purpose in it. I've made my peace with MS, but I know there are still hurdles I have to overcome. The biggest of these is accepting me for who I am now, not living in the past of who I used to be.

The battle I'd been fighting all these years was a dual one. On the surface, I didn't want to accept the diagnosis of MS. When acceptance finally came, a deeper struggle emerged: the battle of feeling comfortable in my own skin. In short, it was fairly easy for me to accept the MS diagnosis when the time was right. It's been much more difficult for me to accept *me*.

It occurs to me that if I'm comfortable in my own skin, it will allow others to be more comfortable around me. That is definitely something I desire.

Once while at a family party, I was conversing with my aunt and telling her that I talk slowly, that I don't hear or see that great—basically my laundry list of MS symptoms. I went on to tell her how uncomfortable I get with people looking at me.

She replied, "Don't worry about them. You are who you are. Who cares?" This was comforting to hear. Not that no one cares about me, but that it doesn't matter what others think when you're comfortable with who you are at the core. It matters what I think of me. I need to accept me as I am now and the rest will fall into place.

Accepting myself has been the fight within the fight. Of course, early on there were reasons to believe my condition might be something other than MS. But as the years dragged on and my condition got worse, I realized that on a deeper level, I was rejecting myself by rejecting the MS diagnosis. I wasn't happy with who I was becoming and wanted a miracle cure to get me back to the way things were before.

How freeing the power of acceptance is. I first had to accept my diagnosis and then accept who I am now because of it.

I don't care anymore about the eyes on me or the MS laundry list. That was more for my benefit than theirs. They could plainly see and hear my impairments. I no longer feel the need to explain or apologize. I've accepted who I am and I don't care about the limitations so much. I care about finding ways around them so that I can really get out and enjoy all that life has to offer. I've declared my independence from self-imposed limits and have finally won the war against inferiority.

Thomas Paine said, "That which we obtain too cheaply, we esteem too lightly."

My freedom didn't come cheaply. I struggled for so long and carried a lot of weight that I didn't need to. I've now learned to cherish each moment, and all of life's small victories. Instead of worrying what people around me are thinking, I'm focusing on enjoying just being with them. Instead of trying to explain away my weaknesses, I'm moving past them and trying to find ways to make them into strengths.

On a recent Oprah show about war veterans, I was struck by what one of the veterans said. Coming back from the war with a disability, she initially thought people had to adjust to her. When the reality of her disability sunk in, she realized that she had to adjust to people. This resonated with me, and I whole heartedly agreed. If you yourself are not comfortable with who you are, who else will be?

Last night I went to bed determined to start anew today. I have fallen into a rut lately: a rut of watching TV without any purpose and really not being productive with my day. My first goal was to watch my Joel Osteen recording (TV with a purpose, if you will). A new one is recorded on my DVR every Sunday. I usually get to it later in the week if at all. First goal accomplished. My second goal is to give a brief synopsis here. The message today was about being happy. That's an easy statement to make, but at times a difficult task to walk out. Abraham Lincoln once said, "Most people are as happy as they decided to be." Easily put, being happy is a choice you have to make every day. Life may be hard for you right now. Maybe you lost your job, perhaps your family has fallen apart, or your health is failing? No matter what, it's your choice. Having or getting the right perspective on your life situations will help you to be happy. I like to think of myself as an overall happy person, but I have those dark moments. When I get there it helps to be thankful for the little things. A quote I heard years ago said, "It's not the outlook that matters, but the uplook." I agree partially with that statement. Yes, keeping your eyes on God is number one, but having a positive outlook is good too. I know just thinking about a positive future has helped get me through. So let's be happy on purpose.

As you've learned by now, I'm not always upbeat and happy. Nor will you be. Note another blog entry that conveys this:

Yesterday was a day for me and Emily to just hang out: breakfast out, a couple hours with our niece and my sister Kim. Later we saw a movie in the theatre and then had dinner. This was our first time seeing a movie at the newer facility at the mall--very handi-friendly. The movie ended up being better than I expected. All that was great. Here's what pissed me off: being in a wheelchair. It's a rare day when I feel this way. I let my mind wander back to my younger, healthier days and thus allowed that PO'd feeling in. Yes, I'd rather be walking, but I'm truly happy where I'm at. I'm always an open book and I really wanted you to see all sides of dealing with disability. As positive and upbeat as I can be I do have a time when I feel defeated once in a while. Having a strong, loving wife as I do makes those down moments easier to get through. I love you Emily!

I have a rule of thumb about wallowing in self-pity: you can go to the dark place, but you can't camp out there. Don't wallow; be happy.

There are many reasons to struggle in life. I'm not sure what yours is. The main thing I wanted to accomplish in telling my story is to extend a "hope-ing hand." I don't know where you are in your journey, but I hope these words can be a hand of comfort on your shoulder, a hand to pull you out of the crap you've been wallowing in, or a hand to boost you up to the higher place you are choosing to live.

LET'S DANCE

This book started with a dream I had, a literal dream that seemed far-fetched, but that really stayed with me like all good dreams do: me atop the Sears Tower, talking people out of ending their lives. There were numerous reasons why they had talked themselves on to the ledge, but one-by-one I encouraged each one and talked them off of it.

I hope that something I've relayed or have lived through has brought you to a hope that you can get down from your ledge and live a happy life.

I can't say this is where I thought I'd always be. As a kid I had dreams of grandeur: President of the United States of America was mine. It started with something so small, the milk lady at lunch calling me Mr. President. Later on, in junior high school, my dream was to be a professional athlete. In high school, my dream shifted to becoming a pastor. Needless to say, I never imagined I'd be here right now: a disabled guy at home with just his thoughts. The reason I get up and keep pushing is because of dreams. Writing a book has been a long-time dream of mine. Check. I think it's good to never stop dreaming. It keeps you going.

> I'm not exactly sure what happened, but I've been motivated a lot more lately. For some time I had felt like a bum. I had not felt the push to be productive. Maybe it took me just making the decision to do something of value with my time. Maybe it's the fact that I'm a husband and I feel the need to be a better man for my wife. Maybe it's because I want to be more than just a pretty face in the crowd. :-) Maybe listening to Matt's album again has just reinforced my desire to do something great with my time. Whatever the reason I'm thankful for that kick in the butt. The maybes aren't that important. I say let's all take our maybe's and do something great.

I've taken great comfort in the words of wisdom that family and friends have shared over the years. A friend of mine shared this once, "Life might not be the party you expected, but since you're here you might as well dance." I may not be the most graceful or skilled dancer, but I intend to make sure my dance card is always full.

And of course, my dad's words have never failed me. He said, "Find what you love and do that." I'm not exactly sure what that is right now, but I'm looking forward to figuring it out, and I'll be blogging along the way. The journey continues at www.randybeal.com.